✧ *Companions for the Journey* ✧

Praying with
Elizabeth Seton

✧ *Companions for the Journey* ✧

Praying with Elizabeth Seton

by
Margaret Alderman
and
Josephine Burns, DC

Saint Mary's Press
Christian Brothers Publications
Winona, Minnesota

To
✧ *Sister Margaret Mary Callahan* ✧
and
✧ *Sister Elizabeth Steiner,* ✧
friends in eternity
MA

✧ *To Mary Valin Burns,* ✧
my mother
JB

Genuine recycled paper with 10% post-consumer waste.
Printed with soy-based ink.

The publishing team for this book included Carl Koch, development editor; Barbara Augustyn Sirovatka, manuscript editor and typesetter; Elaine Kohner, illustrator; pre-press, printing, and binding by the graphics division of Saint Mary's Press.

The acknowledgments continue on page 112.

Printed in the United States of America

Printing: 9 8 7 6 5

Year: 2004 03 02 01

ISBN 0-88489-282-4

✧ Contents ✧

✧ Foreword ✧

Companions for the Journey

Just as food is required for human life, so are companions. Indeed, the word *companions* comes from two Latin words: *com*, meaning "with," and *panis*, meaning "bread." Companions nourish our heart, mind, soul, and body. They are also the people with whom we can celebrate the sharing of bread.

Perhaps the most touching stories in the Bible are about companionship: the Last Supper, the wedding feast at Cana, the sharing of the loaves and the fishes, and Jesus' breaking of bread with the disciples on the road to Emmaus. Each incident of companionship with Jesus revealed more about his mercy, love, wisdom, suffering, and hope. When Jesus went to pray in the Garden of Olives, he craved the companionship of the Apostles. They let him down. But God sent the Spirit to inflame the hearts of the Apostles, and they became faithful companions to Jesus and to each other.

Throughout history, other faithful companions have followed Jesus and the Apostles. These saints and mystics have also taken the journey from conversion, through suffering, to resurrection. Just as they were inspired by the holy people who went before them, so too may you take them as your companions as you walk on your spiritual journey.

The Companions for the Journey series is a response to the spiritual hunger of Christians. This series makes available the rich spiritual teachings of mystics and guides whose wisdom can help us on our pilgrimages. As you complete the last meditation in each volume, it is hoped that you will feel supported, challenged, and affirmed by a soul-companion on your spiritual journey.

The spiritual hunger that has emerged over the last twenty years is a great sign of renewal in Christian life. People fill retreat programs and workshops on topics in spirituality. The demand for spiritual directors exceeds the number available. Interest in the lives and writings of saints and mystics is increasing as people search for models of whole and holy Christian life.

Praying with Elizabeth

Praying with Elizabeth Seton is more than just a book about Elizabeth's spirituality. This book seeks to engage you in praying in the way that Elizabeth did about issues and themes that were central to her experience. Each meditation can enlighten your understanding of her spirituality and lead you to reflect on your own experience.

The goal of *Praying with Elizabeth Seton* is that you will discover Elizabeth's rich spirituality and integrate her spirit and wisdom into your relationship with God, with your brothers and sisters, and with your own heart and mind.

Suggestions for Praying with Elizabeth

Meet Elizabeth Seton, a fascinating companion for your pilgrimage, by reading the introduction to this book, which begins on page 13. It provides a brief biography of Elizabeth and an outline of the major themes of her spirituality.

Once you meet Elizabeth, you will be ready to pray with her and to encounter God, your sisters and brothers, and yourself in new and wonderful ways. To help your prayer, here are some suggestions that have been part of the tradition of Christian spirituality:

Create a sacred space. Jesus said, "When you pray, go to your private room, shut yourself in, and so pray to your [God] who is in that secret place, and your [God] who sees all that is done in secret will reward you" (Matthew 6:6). Solitary prayer is best done in a place where you can have privacy and silence, both of which can be luxuries in the life of busy people.

If privacy and silence are not possible, create a quiet, safe place within yourself, perhaps while riding to and from work, while sitting in line at the dentist's office, or while waiting for someone. Do the best you can, knowing that a loving God is present everywhere. Whether the meditations in this book are used for solitary prayer or with a group, try to create a prayerful mood with candles, meditative music, an open Bible, or a crucifix.

Open yourself to the power of prayer. Every human experience has a religious dimension. All of life is suffused with God's presence. So remind yourself that God is present as you begin your period of prayer. Do not worry about distractions. If something keeps intruding during your prayer, spend some time talking with God about it. Be flexible because God's Spirit blows where it will.

Prayer can open your mind and widen your vision. Be open to new ways of seeing God, people, and yourself. As you open yourself to the Spirit of God, different emotions are evoked, such as sadness from tender memories, or joy from a celebration recalled. Our emotions are messages from God that can tell us much about our spiritual quest. Also, prayer strengthens our will to act. Through prayer, God can touch our will and empower us to live according to what we know is true.

Finally, many of the meditations in this book will call you to employ your memories, your imagination, and the circumstances of your life as subjects for prayer. The great mystics and saints realized that they had to use all their resources to know God better. Indeed, God speaks to us continually and touches us constantly. We must learn to listen and feel with all the means that God has given us.

Come to prayer with an open mind, heart, and will.

Preview each meditation before beginning. After you have placed yourself in God's presence, spend a few moments previewing the readings and especially the reflection activities. Several reflection activities are given in each meditation because different styles of prayer appeal to different personalities or personal needs. **Note that each meditation has more reflection activities than can be done during one prayer period.**

Therefore, select only one or two reflection activities each time you use a meditation. Do not feel compelled to complete all the reflection activities.

Read meditatively. Each meditation offers you a story about Elizabeth and a reading from her writings. Take your time reading. If a particular phrase touches you, stay with it. Relish its feelings, meanings, and concerns.

Use the reflections. Following the readings is a short reflection in commentary form, which is meant to give perspective to the readings. Then you are offered several ways of meditating on the readings and the theme of the prayer. You may be familiar with the different methods of meditating, but in case you are not, they are described briefly here:

✦ *Repeated short prayer or mantra:* One means of focusing your prayer is to use a *mantra,* or "prayer word." The mantra may be a single word or a short phrase taken from the readings or from the Scriptures. For example, the short prayer for meditation 5 in this book is simply the name of Jesus. Repeated slowly in harmony with your breathing, the mantra helps you center your heart and mind on one action or attribute of God.

✦ *Lectio divina:* This type of meditation is "divine studying," a concentrated reflection on the word of God or the wisdom of a spiritual writer. Most often in *lectio divina,* you will be invited to read one of the passages several times and then concentrate on one or two sentences, pondering their meaning for you and their effect on you. *Lectio divina* commonly ends with formulation of a resolution.

✦ *Guided meditation:* In this type of meditation, our imagination helps us consider alternative actions and likely consequences. Our imagination helps us experience new ways of seeing God, our neighbors, ourselves, and nature. When Jesus told his followers parables and stories, he engaged their imagination. In this book, you will be invited to follow guided meditations.

One way of doing a guided meditation is to read the scene or story several times, until you know the outline and can recall it when you enter into reflection. Or before your prayer time, you may wish to record the meditation on a tape recorder. If so, remember to allow pauses for reflection between phrases and to speak with a slow, peaceful pace and tone. Then, during prayer, when you have finished the readings and the reflection commentary, you can turn on your recording of the meditation and be led through it. If you find your own voice too distracting, ask a friend to make the tape for you.

✦ *Examen of consciousness:* The reflections often will ask you to examine how God has been speaking to you in your past and present experience—in other words, the reflections will ask you to examine your awareness of God's presence in your life.

✦ *Journal writing:* Writing is a process of discovery. If you write for any length of time, stating honestly what is on your mind and in your heart, you will unearth much about who you are, how you stand with your God, what deep longings reside in your soul, and more. In some reflections, you will be asked to write a dialog with Jesus or someone else. If you have never used writing as a means of meditation, try it. Reserve a special notebook for your journal writing. If desired, you can go back to your entries at a future time for an examen of consciousness.

✦ *Action:* Occasionally, a reflection will suggest singing a favorite hymn, going out for a walk, or undertaking some other physical activity. Actions can be meaningful forms of prayer.

Using the Meditations for Group Prayer

If you wish to use the meditations for community prayer, these suggestions may help:

✦ Read the theme to the group. Call the community into the presence of God, using the short opening prayer. Invite one or two participants to read one or both readings. If you use both readings, observe the pause between them.

✦ The reflection commentary may be used as a reading, or it can be deleted, depending on the needs and interests of the group.

✦ Select one of the reflection activities for your group. Allow sufficient time for your group to reflect, to recite a centering prayer or mantra, to accomplish a studying prayer *(lectio divina)*, or to finish an examen of consciousness. Depending on the group and the amount of available time, you may want to invite the participants to share their reflections, responses, or petitions with the group.

✦ Reading the passage from the Scriptures may serve as a summary of the meditation.

✦ If a formulated prayer or a psalm is given as a closing, it may be recited by the entire group. Or you may ask participants to offer their own prayers for the closing.

Now you are ready to begin praying with Elizabeth Seton, a faithful and caring companion on this stage of your spiritual journey. It is hoped that you will find her to be a true soul-companion.

CARL KOCH
Editor

Note: The authors have used the most authentic source documents available; many of these are Mother Seton's personal letters. You will notice instances of nonstandard sentence construction, capitalization, punctuation, and even spelling. Because such nonstandard usage in personal correspondence is common for most of us, we have used Mother Seton's letters as they were originally written.

✧ Introduction ✧

Elizabeth Ann Bayley Seton:
An American Original

Elizabeth Seton holds a special place in the story of the Catholic church in America. A wife and widow, mother of five children and of a new community of religious women, teacher and administrator, Elizabeth Seton was remarkable by any standard. Most importantly, Elizabeth Seton was a holy person who companioned other people to a greater love of God and of their sisters and brothers. In recognition of her holiness, on 14 September 1975, Pope Paul VI declared: "Elizabeth Ann Seton . . . is a saint." She is the first saint to grow from the soil of the United States.

After Mother Seton's death, her longtime friend and adviser Father Simon Bruté wrote to another friend of hers:

> Near home we deposited her precious remains on the day following that of her death. In this little wood she reposes with about fifteen Sisters and novices who had come to join her. She leaves more than fifty Sisters to survive her, to regret her and to follow in her footsteps—forty of them at St. Joseph's, the others at the Mountain, in Philadelphia and New York. She lived only for her Sisters and for the performance of her holy duties. She translated for their benefit our best French works, and copied whatever might be useful to the community.
>
> How profound her faith and how tender her piety! How sincere her humility, combined with so great intelligence! How great her goodness and kindness for all!

Her distinguishing characteristic was compassion and indulgence for poor sinners. Her charity made her watchful never to speak evil of others, always to find excuses or to keep silence. Her other special virtues were her attachment to her friends and her gratitude; her religious respect for the ministers of the Lord and for everything pertaining to religion. Her heart was compassionate, religious, lavish of every good in her possession, disinterested in regard to all things.

O Mother, excellent Mother, I trust you are now in the enjoyment of bliss! (Joseph I. Dirvin, *Mrs. Seton*, pp. 454–455)

Indeed, *Mother* serves as the best title for Elizabeth "Betty" Seton—a woman strong and tender, sensitive and determined, nurturing and firm, open and principled—Mother Seton.

Elizabeth's Story

Childhood in New York

Elizabeth Ann Bayley was born on 28 August in 1774, a time when New York boasted of thirty thousand inhabitants and the American colonies were preparing to revolt. Elizabeth's father, Richard Bayley, was a respected physician in the city; her mother, Catherine, was the daughter of an Episcopal rector.

In 1777, Mrs. Bayley died giving birth, leaving Elizabeth and her older sister, Mary, motherless. Richard Bayley remarried in 1778, and the second marriage changed Elizabeth's status in the family and her relationship with her father.

A highly respected physician, Dr. Bayley was frequently called away from home for long periods. The young stepmother, Charlotte, conscientiously cared for Mary and Elizabeth, but she obviously loved her own children more. Solicitous for his young wife, Dr. Bayley focused his attention on his new children. Elizabeth often felt cut off from family closeness. Anxious for her father's affection, she would sometimes dart out of the house, leaving her studies behind, just to kiss her father as he passed by on the street. As a further sign of her marginal membership in the family, at the age of eight, Elizabeth, along with her sister, was sent to live with relatives in the country.

Growing Up

Elizabeth benefited from her time in the country. She developed a keen love of nature and a sense of God's presence. Often lonely, she turned to God for companionship, and it was during this period that she began her lifelong devotion to reading the Bible. In the midst of her reading and musing, her thoughts often turned to memories of her mother and to reflections on death and heaven. Because she lived during an era in which a long life might be only forty or fifty years, dealing with death was a familiar experience for Elizabeth.

Although she had a quiet, reflective side, Elizabeth was also lively and vivacious. As she grew older, she loved to dance, sing, play the piano, and go to the theater.

In 1786, Elizabeth and Mary moved back into the city and their father's house. Elizabeth often took care of her stepbrothers and stepsisters, the oldest of whom was seven. She sang and read to them and discovered joy in helping. Just as she seemed to be settling in, her life suffered from another disruption, the "Doctors' Riot," and Dr. Bayley's subsequent departure to England for further studies.

The Doctors' Riot occurred in April 1788 when people formed mobs after hearing that physicians, Dr. Bayley among them, were using bodies from Potter's Field to teach surgery to medical students at New York Hospital. Wild exaggerations about body snatchers stealing corpses from family plots led to a full-scale riot, during which doctors' homes were ransacked. The authorities called out the militia, shots were fired, and rioters were killed. Although the Bayley house escaped intrusion, it had been surrounded by an angry mob. The experience left everyone in the household shaken. Soon after, Dr. Bayley set sail to England to study new medical procedures.

Elizabeth and Mary were sent back to live with their relatives in the country. Elizabeth missed her father greatly, but Dr. Bayley never wrote to his wife or to any family member during the year that he was away. Although she never lost her loyalty to her father, Elizabeth felt abandoned and sought solace through her attachment to God.

Even after Dr. Bayley returned to New York and Elizabeth returned home, her estrangement from the family continued. She lived for a period of time with her older sister, Mary, and Mary's new husband, and then with relatives on Staten Island.

Over time, Elizabeth and her father began corresponding. He gained a new appreciation for her, and a genuine closeness gradually grew between them. During this time, Elizabeth made some friendships that would last her entire life. Her loyalty and generous affection clearly demonstrates itself in the many letters she wrote to her friends over the years.

Embracing Life

In spite of difficult and lonely times, Elizabeth embraced life with humor and eagerness. She was in her late teens when she met William Magee Seton, the oldest son of a wealthy and distinguished shipping family of New York. They fell in love and married when Elizabeth was nineteen and Will twenty-five.

The young couple took an active role in the New York social scene. President Washington and his wife resided in the city, and diversions were many. Elizabeth especially loved dancing and going to the theater. Her long years of loneliness and estrangement seemed exorcized by the young couple's happiness.

Elizabeth and Will's first child, Anna Maria, was born in May 1795 in their little home on Wall Street and baptized a month later. Calm bliss seemed to fill their lives. After Anna, Elizabeth and Will had four more children: William in 1796, Richard in 1798, Catherine in 1800, and Rebecca in 1802.

Calamity

The year 1798 brought strife to Elizabeth and her family. Will's father injured himself in a fall on ice. His resulting illness caused great anxiety for Will, who would not only inherit the business but also the care of his seven younger brothers and sisters. After Mr. Seton's death, life for Elizabeth and Will changed drastically.

As she prepared to move to the larger Seton home, and while trying to cope with all the new demands made on her, Elizabeth, then pregnant with Richard, became dangerously run-down. Richard's birth proved difficult, and she recovered slowly. An epidemic of yellow fever then broke out in the city, so Elizabeth and the children moved temporarily to a house in the country. Still working in New York, Will came down with a mild attack of the fever. In late fall, the family was finally reunited.

Reverses came steadily upon the Seton's. The "family disease," tuberculosis, had already taken hold in Will. To make matters worse, the shipping business—plagued by piracy and bad investments—failed rapidly. A disastrous shipwreck in 1800 delivered the final blow to the family business, reducing the Setons to near poverty. Will had to declare bankruptcy just before Christmas. Elizabeth tried to bolster everyone's courage, especially that of her despondent husband, and reorient the whole family to a humbler way of life.

The trials served to strengthen the relationship between Elizabeth and Will, and Elizabeth found another source of support in her close friendship with Will's sister Rebecca, whom she called "my soul's sister." Rebecca and Elizabeth prayed, read the Scriptures, and took communion together, finding strength in each other and in their shared faith.

Even though the Setons' financial status had fallen, Rebecca and Elizabeth joined with other women to help the masses of poor people that were coming into New York. John Henry Hobart, a curate of Trinity Episcopal Church, directed the group.

Eventually the Setons moved to a small house in the Battery, close to the water. Then Elizabeth's father died of typhus, which he had contracted while tending sick immigrants. His death shook Elizabeth profoundly. Simultaneously, Will's tuberculosis became pernicious. As he grew sicker, Elizabeth worried about the state of his soul. At last, in the summer of 1803, Will turned to God, thus answering Elizabeth's prayers and mitigating her anxiety.

Discovering Eternity

Elizabeth and Will hit upon a last desperate strategy to alleviate his tuberculosis—a trip to the milder climate of Italy. Through their shipping business, the Setons had formed close ties with the Filicchi family of Livorno (Leghorn), and Will decided to visit them. Elizabeth had to go with him, even though Rebecca, their youngest, was only a year old. She decided to take eight-year-old Anna with them and made plans for the other children to stay with relatives.

Many in the family thought that they had lost their minds, but Elizabeth was desperate. She wrote to her friend Eliza Sadler, called Sad: "You know that I go *fearless*, for you know where, and how strong, is my trust" (Dirvin, *Mrs. Seton,* p. 108). Elizabeth had to do what she could for Will, even though she realized that no hope remained for his ultimate recovery.

They sailed from New York in early October 1803, after a painful farewell from the children. During the seven-week voyage, Will seemed to improve, and Elizabeth began writing a journal intended for her sister-in-law Rebecca on their return. She kept careful track of everything that happened. By the time the ship sailed into Livorno, she felt quite hopeful.

But disappointment awaited them. A yellow fever epidemic had struck New York, and because Will was visibly ill, officials suspected that he might be carrying the disease. The health authorities quarantined the Setons in a *lazaretto,* a cold, stone tower near the entrance to the harbor and used for the detention of those with contagious diseases.

The Filicchis visited through a grating and had warm food brought to the Setons. The stone building grew so cold that Anna had to warm herself by jumping rope. Under such conditions, Will became steadily more ill, only rallying enough to be released with the family on 19 December, a month after their arrival in Italy.

Will died eight days later, having spent his last hours praying with his wife. Elizabeth recorded, "At a quarter past seven on Tuesday morning, 27th December, his soul was released—and mine from a struggle next to death." Provincial law required a hasty burial, so Elizabeth, assisted by two village women, prepared Will's body. "Oh! Oh! Oh! what a day," she wrote (Dirvin, *Mrs. Seton,* pp. 125–126).

A Time of Conversion

The two Filicchi brothers and their families welcomed Elizabeth warmly; Antonio and his wife, Amabilia, became her lifelong friends. They took Elizabeth to see Florence, where the churches overwhelmed her and the devotion of the common people impressed her. Elizabeth's own faith made it possible for her to perceive and wonder at the faith of other people, and she began attending Mass with the Filicchis. She witnessed people's belief in the real presence of Jesus in the Eucharist and thus began a process of questioning and reordering her own faith that would ultimately lead her to Catholicism.

Unexpected delays in sailing for home gave Elizabeth more time to experience the Catholic faith of the Filicchis. Such rituals as the ringing of the bells in the streets, which signaled that the Blessed Sacrament was being carried to the sick, stirred her discernment. By the time she and Anna sailed for home on 8 April 1804, Elizabeth had new friends and many new questions about her faith.

Searching for Light

The reunion with her children and family was joyous, but Elizabeth soon discovered that her sister-in-law Rebecca was dying of tuberculosis. Elizabeth cared for her "soul's sister" during the few remaining days of Rebecca's life. Grief tempered Elizabeth's happy homecoming, and she lost another strong support.

Elizabeth needed financial help at this time, and at first, friends aided her. However, her interest in becoming a Catholic brought on determined opposition from John Henry Hobart, her Episcopal minister, and many of her friends and relatives, who gradually turned away. Some called her deluded and demanded that she read tracts against Catholicism. Elizabeth understood this opposition to Catholicism and the class disparity behind the opposition; most of New York's Catholics were poor Irish immigrants, attending a tiny rundown church.

Antonio Filicchi supplied her with books about Catholicism, and Elizabeth obediently read both views. A period of intense confusion followed, but Elizabeth prayed insistently for God to lead her to the truth and give her courage when she discovered it.

Finally Elizabeth's irresolution disappeared, and she became a Catholic on 14 March 1805. Her first communion seemed to sweep away Elizabeth's doubts completely.

Affection for her former friends persisted, but their cool-ness and condescension hurt her. Henry Hobart warned his parishioners against associating with Elizabeth or supporting the boarding house that she was starting. Although he later re-versed his position, the damage had been done. Elizabeth's venture would soon fail.

Elizabeth's friends, Julia Scott and Catherine Dupleix (called Dué), remained loyal to her throughout this difficult time. Elizabeth grew closer than ever to her sisters-in-law, Ce-cilia and Harriet Seton. Because she had cared for them since their mother died, these two young women looked upon Eliz-abeth almost as a mother and gradually became drawn to Ca-tholicism too.

Reaching the Mountain

These months of trial certainly deepened Elizabeth's faith, but they also deepened her financial difficulties. When Cecilia be-came a Catholic in June 1806, a new storm of opposition against Elizabeth and her sister-in-law followed. Parents with-drew their children from Elizabeth's school, her chief means of support.

With her financial situation becoming steadily more tenu-ous, Elizabeth encountered Father William Dubourg of the So-ciety of Saint Sulpice, who was the founder of Saint Mary's College in Baltimore. After attending a Sunday Mass at Saint Peter's Church at which Dubourg presided, Elizabeth knocked on the door of the breakfast room where he was eating. They talked long and frankly, and at the end of the conversation, Dubourg asked Elizabeth about her plans for the future. She described her concern that her two sons would not receive a proper education and her hope that she could continue her ministry of teaching.

Upon returning to Baltimore, Dubourg discussed various alternatives with Bishop John Carroll, the first U.S. bishop. They invited Elizabeth to come to Baltimore and open a small school. Because Maryland was relatively free of anti-Catholic hostility, she opted for this opportunity. Her sons went ahead to begin their education at Georgetown thanks to the generos-ity of Antonio Filicchi and Bishop Carroll.

Accompanied by her daughters, Anna, Rebecca, and Kit, Elizabeth left her beloved New York on 9 June 1808. The long months of opposition in New York had deepened her trust in God and prepared her for the new chapter of her life about to unfold.

Baltimore

Guided by Bishop John Carroll, the heart of the Catholic church in the United States was in Baltimore in the early 1800s. A group of Sulpician priests that had escaped the French Revolution assisted Bishop Carroll. When the Setons moved to Baltimore, approximately seventy priests were caring for between seventy and ninety-five thousand Catholics in the entire country.

Elizabeth and her children moved into a little house on Paca Street. When her school finally began in the fall, Elizabeth had seven pupils: four boarders and her own three daughters. Meanwhile, her sons had returned from Georgetown to study at Saint Mary's, close to home.

In a letter to Antonio Filicchi, Elizabeth mentioned the possibility of forming a community of women religious: "It is proposed to . . . begin on a small plan admitting of enlargement if necessary, in the hope and expectation that there will not be wanting ladies to join in forming a permanent institution." Elizabeth did not push this plan, but waited for Providence to lead her. Events moved quickly, and Cecilia O'Conway, "the first of Mother Seton's daughters and 'Philadelphia's first nun'" came to join her in December 1808 (Dirvin, *Mrs. Seton*, pp. 221, 225).

Samuel S. Cooper, a wealthy seminarian, gave ten thousand dollars to help Elizabeth establish a religious community, stipulating that the foundation be at Emmitsburg, Maryland, a small settlement in a lovely valley some fifty miles west of Baltimore. Bishop Carroll appointed Elizabeth to be superior of the new community and received her first vows on 25 March 1809. After that day, Elizabeth was called Mother Seton.

Other young women came to join Elizabeth and Cecilia O'Conway, and on 2 June 1809, the sisters came to Mass imitating Elizabeth's style of dress, the dress of a widow—a black dress with a leather belt from which hung a rosary; a short cape; and a white muslin cap. Some days later, Harriet and Cecilia Seton joined the community.

Emmitsburg

Even though the house at Emmitsburg was not quite ready, Elizabeth, Anna, Maria Murphy, and Harriet and Cecilia Seton set out for their new home in the mountains. Except for Cecilia, who was ill, all walked beside their covered wagon. On the fourth day, 21 June 1809, they reached their destination.

Emmitsburg was already home to Saint Joseph's Church and Mount Saint Mary's College for boys. Father John Dubois headed the little college and presided as pastor of the village church. By the end of July, the whole community, now called Sisters of Charity of Saint Joseph, had assembled in Emmitsburg.

The little Stone House that they inhabited had only two rooms on the ground floor and two in the attic. The sisters had to lay their mattresses on the floor and did not have enough dishes to go around. Elizabeth, her five children, Cecilia and Harriet Seton, eight sisters, two pupils from the Paca Street school, and the young son of Sister Rose White, a widow like Elizabeth, all lived in the small house. In the fall, the boys would go to school at Mount Saint Mary's, but a larger residence, eventually called the White House, was begun at once by Father Dubois and the men of the parish.

Life gradually settled into a routine of regular spiritual exercises in the community and work with the children in school. But the community soon experienced its first test. Father William Dubourg resigned as the community's director, and Father John Baptist David, the spiritual adviser of Sister Rose White, was appointed in his place. From the beginning of his term, Father David did his utmost to replace Elizabeth with Sister Rose as Superior.

David assumed that he should exercise complete control over the community, and Elizabeth and her council immediately found themselves in the midst of a divisive conflict. After trying unsuccessfully to work with David, Elizabeth took the case of her community to Archbishop Carroll, explaining her position honestly, patiently, and without bitterness. She waited obediently for the bishop's decision, but time dragged on, and ultimately Father David had charge of the order for two years. His arrogance and the resulting divisions in the community pained Elizabeth greatly, but she showed little of her distress outwardly. Finally David was replaced, and Elizabeth once more regained the direction of the community.

During this time of tension, both Harriet and Cecilia Seton died: Harriet of a sudden brain fever and Cecilia of tuberculosis. With their deaths, Elizabeth lost two longtime friends and allies.

The Rule of Life

From their inception, the Sulpician Fathers had close ties with Vincent de Paul and the Daughters of Charity in France. Because Bishop Carroll had appointed the Sulpicians as the ecclesiastical superiors of the Emmitsburg sisters, they naturally urged the sisters to model themselves after the French Daughters of Charity. Consequently, the Rule of the Daughters of Charity was adapted for the community at Emmitsburg. As early as January 1810, Mother Seton mentions this connection in a letter to Eliza Sadler: "If you recollect the system of the Sisters of Charity . . . in France, you will know the rule of our community in a word, which amounts only to that regularity necessary for order and no more" (Dirvin, *Mrs. Seton*, p. 272).

Father David actually sought to bring Daughters of Charity from France and unite the two communities. With this in mind, he asked another Sulpician, Benedict Flaget, to bring back a copy of the Rule and constitutions of the French community and to arrange for Daughters of Charity to come to Emmitsburg to instruct the American sisters in religious life. Because France was in turmoil due to Napoleon's adventures, the Daughters could not leave France. The Rule and constitutions did make their way to America and were adapted by Elizabeth Seton and her community. Archbishop Carroll approved the permanent rules of the Emmitsburg Sisters of Charity on 11 September 1811.

The Early Years of the Community

Life for the community in Emmitsburg was difficult. The sisters had little income, and their housing was spartan. The cold winters took their toll, but the work prospered with Elizabeth at the helm.

The community rose at 5:00 a.m., said morning prayer, meditated, attended Mass, and then had breakfast. At 9:00 a.m., the community prayed an act of adoration. They worked until 11:45 a.m. and then made an examination of conscience and read the Scriptures. A brief recreation period followed lunch. At 2:00 p.m., the sisters gathered to hear the *Imitation of Christ*, to read, and to pray. They worked again until 5:00 p.m., at which time they recited the rosary. During supper, they listened to spiritual readings. The community recreated until 8:30 p.m., said night prayer, and went to bed.

Besides teaching and other ministerial duties, the sisters cleaned, sewed, tended their own garden, and did their laundry—a daylong project in itself. One of the sisters described doing the laundry: "Our washing place was at the creek where we took our clothes early in the morning and remained all day. Not a plank to stand on, not a covering but the tree under which we placed our tubs" (Dirvin, *Mrs. Seton*, p. 251). Their lives were balanced between work, prayer, and recreation. Like those of most women of the time, their lives were hard.

Nevertheless, the community grew. The school at Saint Joseph's became a parish school and is now considered the beginning of the Catholic parochial school system in the United States.

Going Home

Tuberculosis ravaged the community. The death of her eldest daughter, in particular, nearly crushed Elizabeth. Anna had accompanied Elizabeth and Will to Italy, and she held a special place in Elizabeth's heart. Anna had spent some time living in Baltimore, but she found herself lonely and unhappy while away from the community. Subsequently she entered the little community formally, but lived only a short while as a sister, dying a few months before her seventeenth birthday. The sorrow over Anna's death never left Elizabeth, even though she soon accepted it as part of God's plan for her.

More leave-taking was in store. Rebecca, Elizabeth's youngest child, fell on the ice and badly injured her hip. Not wanting to cause trouble, she did not tell her mother and tried to walk as straight as possible, further aggravating the injury. Permanent damage resulted. Despite close attention from physicians, her condition grew worse, and tuberculosis settled in the injured joint. Rebecca died in her mother's arms on 3 November 1816; she was only fourteen years old.

Elizabeth was losing her own battle with tuberculosis. The trials of separation, conflict, and death had worn on her. In addition, Elizabeth worried about her children. Her sons' careers remained unsettled; she sent William, and later Richard, to learn business with the Filicchis in Italy, but both proved inept. William insisted on a naval career, and Elizabeth used her contacts to obtain a commission for him. Eventually, Richard went the way of his older brother, but Elizabeth fretted about their instability and frequent silences. Concerned that her daughter, Kit (Catherine Josephine), needed experience outside the valley, Elizabeth sent her to visit friends and relatives.

The Last Illness

The summer of 1820 marked the beginning of Elizabeth's last illness. She began to feel much weaker; pain and coughing attacked her more persistently and powerfully. Near the end of August, Elizabeth was forced to her bed with a fever. Nonetheless, she followed the exercises and rules of the community as closely as she could. She rallied for days at a time, but the end was obviously coming. Even when burning with fever, she refused to take any water during the night if she were to receive Holy Communion in the morning. (At that time, drinking water after midnight broke the required eucharistic fast.)

As the new year of 1821 began, the sister on watch urged Mother Seton to take her medicine, but she refused, saying, "Never mind the drink. One Communion more—and then eternity" (Dirvin, *Mrs. Seton,* p. 453). Early on the morning of 4 January 1821, Elizabeth died peacefully.

Her Work Continues

Mother Seton's community spread rapidly. During her life, the sisters took over orphanages in Philadelphia and New York, and a German parish school in Philadelphia. Eventually, Sisters of Charity would minister throughout North America.

In 1846, a group of the Emmitsburg sisters working in New York City separated from the original motherhouse to form the Sisters of Charity of Saint Vincent de Paul of New York. From this branch came two other groups: the Sisters of Charity of Halifax (1856), and the Sisters of Charity of Saint Elizabeth, Convent Station, New Jersey (1859). In 1852, Emmitsburg sisters working in the Archdiocese of Cincinnati formed a separate community. In 1870, from this same group came the Mother Seton Sisters of Charity of Greensburg, Pennsylvania. Several other communities of Sisters of Charity also take Elizabeth Seton as their inspiration and guide.

Meanwhile, the affiliation of the Emmitsburg sisters with the French community of Daughters of Charity of Saint Vincent de Paul came to fruition in 1850. Elizabeth had translated the lives of Vincent de Paul and Louise de Marillac, co-founders of the Daughters of Charity, for community use, and in those early days, spoke affectionately of the French community as "our European Sisters" (Dirvin, *Mrs. Seton,* p. 305). Thus the Daughters of Charity in America today also call her Mother Seton.

Praying with Elizabeth Seton

Naturally, Elizabeth's spirituality grew with her experiences as wife and mother, teacher and foundress, convert and community member. Like all people—saints and sinners—she was a person of her times, so her attitudes and approaches reflect her times. Nevertheless, she can be a wonderful and inspiring companion for spiritual pilgrims today. Her spirituality has the following characteristics:

Trust in the Scriptures

Elizabeth regularly read and prayed with the Scriptures. She took them seriously, referring to the word of God when she needed to make crucial decisions and then acting on the message she found there.

Holding Fast to Faith

Given the amount of suffering in her life, it would have been understandable if Elizabeth had fallen into bitterness or despair. What held her up and kept her going was her tremendous faith in God's unconditional love for her. She also held fast to her belief that doing God's will would lead her to greater love and firmer hope. In short, Elizabeth Seton's faith gave her supreme confidence that ultimately all would be well. Her faith was sustained by prayer and by nourishment of the Eucharist.

Centrality of Love

For Elizabeth, doing God's will meant loving. She understood the love found in intimate friendships. Indeed, she treasured her friends and maintained those friendships through her voluminous correspondence and constant solicitude.

She models nurturing love through her devotion as a parent and teacher. Elizabeth shows us the unselfish love that Jesus calls Christians to have toward enemies. Many times in her life, the demands of love called her to leave security and comfort, but she knew that by loving—doing God's will—she would be rewarded by greater love. In choosing the name Sisters of Charity, Elizabeth signaled to her followers that love should be the central focus of their lives.

Dignity of Parenting

By her own description, parenting her children was not only a key obligation for Elizabeth but a defining part of her way of following Jesus. For Mother Seton, no dichotomy existed between being a mother and giving herself to God. She loved her children totally and thanked God for them. Mary, the mother of Jesus, provided Elizabeth with an inspiration and example, and she turned to Mary frequently for solace and guidance.

Hope in the Resurrection

Mother Seton and death were intimately acquainted. Death took Elizabeth's husband, two of her children, several of the sisters in her community, and many of her friends before it finally stopped for her. She understood grief as only someone who has so often experienced it can. However, hope in the final, glorious resurrection promised by Jesus' own rising sustained her optimism and gave her strength to go on.

Mother Seton for Today

Married couples, parents, especially single parents, will likely find a kindred spirit in Mother Seton. As a loyal and trusted friend, Elizabeth's great love and hopeful spirit can still reach out to sustain and nourish people living in her much-changed homeland. Mother Seton was a mother to her children, her students, and her community. She was also a "soul's sister" to her friends. Perhaps she can be your mothering spirit and a sister to your soul.

✧ Meditation 1 ✧

God's Word in the Heart

Theme: Elizabeth often spoke of God's word as her "dear Scripture" and approached every event of her life with reference to biblical teachings.

Opening prayer: I pray that your word, O God, may be written in my heart and in my mind.

About Elizabeth

As a child baptized and spiritually nourished in the Episcopal church, Elizabeth was instructed in the King James Bible. The verses and phrases came easily to her mind as she went about her daily living. During her teen years, her father traveled for a long period. New Rochelle relatives took care of her, and during this time she truly opened herself to God's loving influence. Experiencing deep loneliness, she wandered the fields and walked by the sea, where she spoke with God and pondered the Scriptures.

Throughout her life, Bible reading was a principal source for Elizabeth's comfort, for the wisdom she imparted to her husband and children, and for conferences with the Sisters of Charity. Elizabeth set aside time for reading by rising early each day. This simple comment in her journals typifies the place of Bible reading in her day: "The sun was bright and I was seated in the open air, and I read my Bible for two hours" (Madame de Barberey, *Elizabeth Seton*, p. 31).

On another occasion, Elizabeth remarked:

I have just passed one of the most pleasant evenings of my life. It is now eleven o'clock and I have been sitting here since seven with my book, which has spoken to me of the Most High and the Most Holy, who remains forever. I have selected here and there, and copied passages which I like to preserve for my daughter. How small the world seems when one looks at it from a distance! These are calm and peaceful hours, thus spent in solitude; they are valuable for their good advice, and the memory of them endures. (De Barberey, *Elizabeth Seton*, p. 31)

Pause: Ponder this question: Is reading the Scriptures woven into my daily occupations, both in good times and in bad?

Elizabeth's Words

While Will, Anna, and Elizabeth Seton were quarantined in the *lazaretto*, a damp, stone tower at the entrance of Livorno harbor used for the detention of those with contagious diseases, they suffered physical inconvenience and emotional torment. Friends feared that Elizabeth would lose her reason shut up in that prison, and they told her so by letter.

True to her nature, Elizabeth made the best of the situation, encouraging and supporting her husband and their daughter in that place of exile, and relying on her lifelong devotion to the Scriptures. She wrote:

Finished reading the Testament through, which we began the sixth of October, and my Bible as far as Ezekiel, which I have always read to myself in rotation, but the lessons appointed in the prayer book to my William. Today read him several passages in Isaiah which he enjoyed so much that he was carried for a while out of his troubles. Indeed, our reading is an unfailing comfort. (Ellin M. Kelly, comp. and ed., *Numerous Choirs*, p. 71)

In another journal entry, Elizabeth commented:

Enjoyments only come when all is quiet and I have passed an hour or two with King David, the Prophet Isaiah; those hours, I often think, I shall hereafter esteem the most precious of my life. My Father and my God, who by the consoling voice of His word builds up the soul in hope, so as to free it even for hours of its incumbrance, confirming and strengthening it by the constant experience of his indulgent goodness, giving it a new life in Him, even while in the midst of pains and sufferings. (De Barberey, *Elizabeth Seton*, p. 62)

Reflection

We do not always have access to spiritual directors or wise people to counsel us in times of confusion or doubt. When Elizabeth wanted to know what Jesus would do, she turned her mind and heart to the Scriptures. Reading them gave her direction and confidence.

In her journals, Elizabeth made it clear that she regularly spent time studying and praying with God's word. The Scriptures helped her cope with the many trials of her life: the death of her husband, poverty, rejection by family and old friends, and the loss of many loved ones. She let the word of God touch her heart and guide her will.

✧ Read "Elizabeth's Words" again, slowly and meditatively. Choose a phrase that somehow strikes you as especially meaningful and pray this phrase repeatedly, letting its meaning become clear to you.

✧ Take your Bible into your hands, holding it carefully. Feel the texture of its cover. Think of the person who gave it to you or the time and place in which you obtained it for yourself. Remember times you have opened this book and taken its words into your heart, special times when its words consoled you, challenged you, or affirmed you.

✧ Suppose you had never seen a Bible or heard the words of the Scriptures? How would your life be different? Try to list all the ways that the word of God has helped form your way of living.

✧ One way of praying with the Scriptures is outlined here. Use this method of *lectio divina* (holy study) to pray "God's Word" in this meditation or some other favorite passage from the Bible:
1. Pray a simple act of faith, thanksgiving, and praise to focus or center yourself.
2. Read aloud the scriptural passage, slowly and clearly.
3. Slowly repeat over and over again one line that catches your attention, letting its meaning become more clear.
4. Aloud, read the passage again slowly.
5. Offer a prayer in response to the word, phrase, or line that you find most significant.
6. Again, slowly read aloud the passage.
7. Ponder this question: How do these words of God touch my life at this particular time?
8. End by reciting the Lord's Prayer.

If you find this approach to prayer helpful, you may want to use it again in subsequent meditations in this book.

✧ Reflect on this question: How do I or can I make the study of, and prayer with, the Scriptures an integral part of my spiritual journey?

✧ Relax, and then pray these words from Psalm 19:8:

Your precepts, Yahweh, are right,
they gladden the heart.
Your command is clear,
it gives light to the eyes.

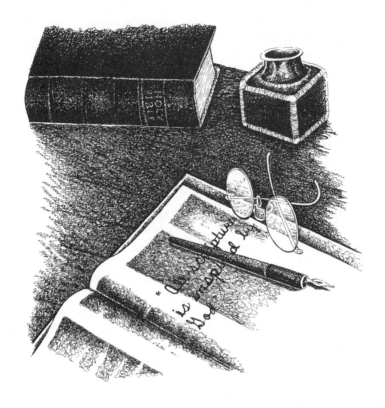

God's Word

You must keep to what you have been taught and know to be true; remember who your teachers were, and how, ever since you were a child, you have known the holy scriptures—from these you can learn the wisdom that leads to salvation through faith in Christ Jesus. All scripture is inspired by God and useful for refuting error, for guiding people's lives and teaching them to be upright. This is how someone who is dedicated to God becomes fully equipped and ready for any good work. (2 Timothy 3:14–17)

Closing prayer: Gracious God, prepare my heart to receive the wisdom and power of the Scriptures and fill my heart with earnest love of your word.

✧ Meditation 2 ✧

Acting on God's Word

Theme: Not only did Elizabeth find God's word consoling and wise, but she believed that we can never be misled when we act with complete faith in God's word. God is forever faithful.

Opening prayer: I pray with Elizabeth Seton for the grace to hear what God says and to stake my life on God's word as she did.

About Elizabeth

In the months before Elizabeth's conversion to the Catholic faith, she was greatly torn by anxiety and doubt over whether she should leave the Episcopal church of her birth. Family, friends, and advisers were almost unanimous in trying to dissuade her. Her Episcopal pastor, Reverend John Henry Hobart, who viewed the Roman Catholic church as evil and dissolute, reminded Elizabeth of her obligation to her children for whom she would have to answer in judgment. This truth at last drove Elizabeth to the point of choice. She wrote to a dear friend that if faith was so important she would "seek it where true Faith first began, seek it among those who received it from GOD HIMSELF" (Dirvin, *Mrs. Seton*, p. 163).

Admitting that she had no ability to solve the controversies, Elizabeth determined to take the Scriptures literally and

to base her actions completely on God's word. In the journal
written for her friend, Amabilia Filicchi, she said:

> May God accept my intention, and pity me. . . .
>
> Come then, my little ones, we will go to judgment to-
> gether, and present Our Lord His own words; and if He
> says, "You fools, I did not mean that," we will say, "Since
> You said You would be *always* even to the end of ages, be
> with this church you built with Your Blood—if You ever
> left it, it is *Your Word* which misled us. Therefore, please
> to pardon Your poor fools for Your own word's sake.
> (Dirvin, *Mrs. Seton*, pp. 163–164)

Pause: Ponder Elizabeth's reliance on God's word as the
expression of God's faithfulness.

Elizabeth's Words

> But, O my God! . . . Your word is truth and without
> contradiction wherever it is! One faith, one hope, one bap-
> tism, I look for wherever it is, and I often think my sins,
> my miseries, hide the light. Yet will I cling to my God to
> the last, begging for that light, and never change until I
> find it. (De Barberey, *Elizabeth Seton*, p. 110)

Reflection

Many situations in our world raise troubling questions for us.
We may find ourselves, like Elizabeth, battered on every side
by well-meaning believers, each proclaiming that his or her
view is the one sensible way to proceed. Some people have
forsaken all hope of finding truth that will give purpose to
their life.

Far from being naive and intimate with suffering, Elizabeth held fast to God's word not only as a source of consolation and direction but also as a guarantee of God's faithfulness
when she acted on the word. Indeed, Elizabeth recognized that
the whole Bible is the story of God's faithfulness to people

who try to do God's will. Thus, when she acted, she did so
with trust that God journeyed with her.

Each day we face decisions. At times, the consequences of
these decisions can be far-reaching, affecting life, death, and
happiness for ourselves and our loved ones. At such times, we
too need to find the truth. Elizabeth would urge us to search
for God's will in the Scriptures, to trust in the answers found
there, and then to trust in God's grace when we act.

✧ Pray slowly and repeatedly Elizabeth's words: "O my
God! . . . Your word is truth."

✧ Pick and ponder a favorite passage of the Scriptures
that has been a guide, a comfort, or a strong support in times
of uncertainty. Why has it meant so much to you? Recall the
circumstances that revealed this passage to you. How has this
passage led you to action? How has acting in light of God's
word in this passage led you to belief in God's love and faithfulness? Take a moment for thanksgiving and praise.

✧ Let a situation or problem troubling you surface in
your consciousness. Who is involved? What are the factors?
What is at stake? Try to lay out the situation or problem completely in God's sight, like an open book. Tell God: "Here it is."
Then search the Scriptures for God's word to you about this
situation or problem; be open to passages that challenge you
to new perspectives as well as to passages that affirm you. Listen to God's word. Ask God to open your heart to truth and to
lead your will in right action. End by making an act of faith in
God's grace.

✧ Recall a time when you were in a room with loved
ones close to you, but you did not communicate vocally with
them. Did you feel their closeness and understanding even
without words—perhaps in a glance or just by being there
with them?

God's presence is often made known in this way—just as
Elijah perceived God in the gentle wind (1 Kings 19:12). Ask
God to open your heart, so that God's love may come in gen-
tly. You may feel God's presence, or you may not. We are not

usually aware of our heartbeats, but that lack of awareness does not change the reality. God is present. Then, using the eight-step process of holy study outlined on page 33 of this book, pray the following "God's Word."

God's Word

For, as the rain and the snow come down from the sky
and do not return before having watered the earth,
fertilising it and making it germinate
to provide seed for the sower and food to eat,
so it is with the word that goes from my mouth:
it will not return to me unfulfilled
or before having carried out my good pleasure
and having achieved what it was sent to do.

(Isaiah 55:10–11)

Closing prayer: God, "I have faith. Help my lack of faith!" (Mark 9:25).

✧ **Meditation 3** ✧

Commitment in Faith

Theme: Elizabeth's faith made her commitment to God's service entire and unassailable.

Opening prayer: God, grant me faith so that I may bless you both in my successes and in the midst of my failures.

About Elizabeth

After Elizabeth became a Catholic, she suffered from the outright hostility and disapproval of some of her relatives and former friends. Such hostility and disapproval not only hurt her personally but also made it difficult for Elizabeth to recruit and keep students at her boarding house. At one point, her lifelong friend and supporter Antonio Filicchi became so concerned that he wrote the company of John Murray and Sons as follows:

> Gentlemen: Christian religion founded in charity is so well understood by some of your neighbors, as to allow themselves the privilege of substituting vexation and persecution to the consolation and relief due to virtue in distress. I refer to my most respected convert, my virtuous, unfortunate friend, Mrs. W. M. Seton, as the persecuted person. The persecutors are her relations, her pretended friends; and religion, in the shocking inconsistency of their brains, is the pretense for vexation. . . .

In addition to the order left with you on my departure from America, you are requested to furnish Mrs. Seton with whatever farther sum she might at any time call for to support herself and family. (Dirvin, *Mrs. Seton,* p. 196)

For her part, Elizabeth stood firm in her faith. Indeed, in a letter to Antonio, now back home in Italy, she said:

3 times a week I beg for you with my whole Soul in the *hour of favour* when nothing is denied to Faith—imagine your poor little wandering erring Sister standing on the Rock, and admitted so often to the spring of *Eternal Life* the healing balm of every wound, indeed if I wore a galling chain and lived on bread and water I ought to feel the *transport* of grace, but Peace of Mind and a sufficient share of exterior comfort *with the inexhaustible Treasure* keeps My Soul in a state of constant comparison between the Giver, and receiver, the former days and the present, and Hope always awake wispers Mercy for the future, as sure as the past. (Ellin Kelly and Annabelle Melville, eds., *Elizabeth Seton: Selected Writings,* p. 199)

Pause: Ask yourself: Do I believe that "nothing is denied to Faith?"

Elizabeth's Words

In a journal from 1802, Elizabeth declared:

It is true the Journey is long, the burthen is heavy—but the Lord delivers his faithful servants from all their troubles—and sometimes even here allows them some hours of sweetest Peace as the earnest of eternal blessedness—Is it nothing to sleep serene under his guardian wing—to awake to the brightness of the glorious sun with renewed strength and renewed blessings—to be blessed with the power of instant communion with the Father of our Spirits the sense of his presence—the influences of his love— to be assured of that love is enough to tie us faithfully to him and while we have fidility to him all the surrounding cares and contradictions of this Life are but Cords of mercy to send us faster to Him. (Kelly and Melville, *Selected Writings*, p. 85)

In another place she said: "Why, Faith lifts the staggering soul on one side, Hope supports it on the other. Experience says it must be, and Love says—let it be" (Joseph B. Code, *Letters of Mother Seton to Mrs. Julianna Scott*, p. 197).

Reflection

Prayer, the Eucharist, the Scriptures, the splendors of creation, supportive friends such as Antonio Filicchi, and spiritual directors informed and strengthened Elizabeth's faith. In turn, her faith gave her the courage to convert, to move to Emmitsburg, to found a community of religious women, and to bear the sufferings of her life.

Elizabeth Seton's convictions were rooted in a profound faith in God's love. The turmoil and traumas of her life turned her to the One Being she could never mistrust and who would never abandon her. Because she took God as the ground and foundation for all her actions, even when people persecuted or turned their backs on her, she held fast to her principles and decisions. She believed and acted upon the conviction that "nothing is denied to Faith."

✧ Slowly and meditatively read "Elizabeth's Words" again. You may want to read them several times. If a word or phrase strikes you as especially important, stay with it until the meaning becomes clearer.

✧ Pray repeatedly these words of Mother Seton: "Nothing is denied to Faith."

✧ Ponder these questions; if you find writing helpful, record your answers in journal form, much as Mother Seton did:

✦ How important is my faith to me?

✦ When has my belief been a rock of strength in a time of trouble?
✦ How do I nurture my faith?
✦ How do I feel about sharing my faith with other people?

✧ Consider what life might bring tomorrow. List five people with whom you will interact and five activities in which you will engage. Next to each name and activity, describe how you should behave if you are motivated by faith in Jesus Christ.

✧ Inventory any sources of anxiety or doubt that bother you. Then relax your body by deep breathing and stretching. Bring yourself into Jesus' presence by imagining that you have invited him to come to your home. He rings your doorbell, and you greet him, welcoming him to sit in your most comfortable chair. After offering Jesus cookies and coffee, tea, or something cool to drink, you talk with him about your worries and questions. He has come just for this conversation with you. Ask him for the gift of faith. As he stands to leave, he embraces you, saying, "Peace I leave with you, my friend."

✧ Sing the hymn "Amazing Grace," offering it to God as a confession of faith.

> Amazing grace, how sweet the sound
> that saved a wretch like me.
> I once was lost, but now I'm found;
> was blind, but now I see.
>
> 'Twas grace that taught my heart to fear,
> and grace my fear relieved.
> How precious did that grace appear
> the hour I first believed.
>
> Thru many dangers, toils and snares
> we have already come.
> 'Twas grace that brought us safe this far,
> and grace will bring us home.
>
> (John Newton)

God's Word

So even those whom God allows to suffer should commit themselves to a Creator who is trustworthy, and go on doing good. (1 Peter 4:19)

Closing prayer: "O my God! Imprint it on my soul with the strength of the Holy Spirit that, by His grace supported and defended, I may never more forget that Thou art my all. . . . Oh, keep me for the sake of Jesus Christ!" (De Barberey, *Elizabeth Seton*, p. 43).

✧ **Meditation 4** ✧

God's Love for Us

Theme: Elizabeth was so confident of God's faithful love that she accepted her trials and difficulties as signs of that love.

Opening prayer: I pray for the wisdom to see all things in my life as calls to confidence in God's ever-present love.

About Elizabeth

In 1808, Elizabeth and her three daughters—the two boys were away at boarding school—traveled by sea from New York to their new life in Baltimore. During the seven-day voyage, the children became dreadfully seasick and restless, and Elizabeth had her hands full caring for them. When they finally saw the harbor, Elizabeth recorded these memories:

> After rolling and dashing all night . . . with both little dear ones in my narrow berth, the hand held over to Ann who sleeps beneath me—praying every ten minutes and offering a life so justly forfeited—here we were flying up the Chesapeake. A fairer wind and lighter hearts never went through it, I believe. The girls are singing, and eating almonds and raisins—sending ships overboard to New York.

Tomorrow, do I go among strangers? No. Has an anxious thought or fear passed my mind? No. Can I be disappointed? No. One sweet Sacrifice [the Eucharist] will reunite my soul with all who offer it. Doubt and fear fly from the breast inhabited by *Him*. There can be no disappointment where the soul's only desire and expectation is to meet *His* Adored Will and fulfill it. (Dirvin, *Mrs. Seton*, p. 212)

This same confidence in God's care remained with Elizabeth throughout her life, even when she was concerned about her often unsettled sons, William and Richard. At one point near the end of her life, she received an infrequent, but long-awaited, letter from Richard. She wrote to a friend:

[He is] full of schemes about settling on the Black River—black indeed will it be to him if he carries it through. He says, "Commerce is a dead loss of time at present." Poor fellow, I fear his faith is dead by the whole tenor of his letters; yet he puts change aside till another year. So, we will see. Nothing from William. You hear my sighs, and they go to your dear heart, I know; but never mind, my Ellen, Our God will pity. (Dirvin, *Mrs. Seton*, p. 439)

Pause: Reflect on this question: How has confidence in God's love lifted me out of the turmoil of a situation?

Elizabeth's Words

During her father's last illness, Elizabeth wrote to her sister-in-law Rebecca: "The Father in heaven is the only solace left to your sister. He never withdraws Himself. Oh, how sweet is such a solace at this time" (De Barberey, *Elizabeth Seton*, p. 36).

During the long agony of her husband's dying, Elizabeth penned these reflections:

Dear indulgent Father, could I be alone, while clinging fast to Thee in continual prayer or thanksgiving? Prayer for him, and joy, wonder, and delight to feel that what I had so fondly hoped and confidently expected really proved in the hour of trial to be more than I could hope, more than I could conceive; that my God could and would hear me through the most severe trials, with that strength, confidence, and affiance [trust] which, if every circumstance of the case was considered, seemed more than a human being could expect or hope. But His consolations! Who shall speak them? How can utterance be given to that which only His Spirit can feel? (De Barberey, *Elizabeth Seton*, p. 64)

When painfully ill herself, Elizabeth remarked: "Sickness does not frighten the secret peace of mind which is founded on a confidence in the divine goodness, and if death succeeds it, I must put a mother's hopes and fears in His hands Who has promised most to the widow and the fatherless" (Dirvin, *Mrs. Seton*, p. 218).

Reflection

We have confidence in a person when our experience has taught us that the person is trustworthy. Confidence is not usually born overnight but results from a long, slow building process. Elizabeth's confidence in God's love began early and grew throughout her life, despite all the trials she underwent. Her regular prayer and reading of the Scriptures nourished her relationship with God and thus her trust in divine love. Her great love for her human father became easily associated with God, whom she readily called Father. Also, Elizabeth's many friends affirmed her trust in God's care, and in turn, she showed them that God could be counted on in all circumstances.

This confidence in God provided the rock on which Elizabeth stood throughout the storms of her life. It can also be a rock for us, and it can be a gift we give to others.

✧ Meditate on "Elizabeth's Words." What challenges do they offer you? How can they be consoling?

✧ Assess your own ability to trust yourself, other people, and God. Reflect on each of the following questions and, if you find writing helpful, jot down your reactions:

✦ When I was young, did I feel that I could trust my parents?
✦ Looking back, did I learn in some fundamental ways that most people could be trusted?
✦ Do I have confidence in my own goodness, lovableness, and ability to love other people?
✦ Which people in my present life give me confidence and help me trust in God, other people, and myself?
✦ When have I experienced God as trustworthy?
✦ How much do I trust that God loves me and has my best interests in mind?
✦ How have I developed my trust in God: Through prayer? Through trusting relationships with other people? Through praying with the Scriptures?

✧ List some situations in your life right now over which you have little control, but about which you experience anxiety. Talk to God about each situation and offer it into God's care. After doing this, pray "Let go, let God."

✧ Pray for an increase in trust by repeating slowly and meditatively Elizabeth's words: "Could I be alone, while clinging fast to Thee?"

✧ Sing a favorite hymn in thanksgiving for God's care.

✧ Pray for single mothers and fathers with whom you are acquainted. Reflect on ways in which you might support and affirm them.

God's Word

Such is the confidence we have through Christ in facing God; it is not that we are so competent that we can claim any credit for ourselves; all our competence comes from God. (2 Corinthians 3:4–5)

Closing prayer: Faithful God, bring me so close to you that all my strength and confidence are in harmony with your designs and your love.

✧　**Meditation 5**　✧

Prayer Without Ceasing

Theme: Often lonely as a child and thrown on her own resources, Elizabeth developed a habit of prayer with which she faced every changing circumstance of life.

Opening prayer: Teach me, O God, such constancy in prayer that it fosters an unending dialog with you.

About Elizabeth

Early in her life, Elizabeth experienced the loss of her mother and the frequent absence of her physician father. She learned to seek God as her comfort and mainstay. One of her favorite places to pray was in nature, where she often found spiritual strength and reassurance. Long walks alone, gazing at the trees at the water's edge and the beautiful countryside of New Rochelle, provided the necessary peace for an eight-year-old's reflections. She wrote: "Every little leaf and flower, or insect, animal, shades of clouds, or waving trees were objects of vacant unconnected thoughts of God and heaven" (Rose Maria Laverty, *Loom of Many Threads*, p. 118). In short, as a child, she learned to pray her experiences.

As her life spun on, Elizabeth turned more constantly to God, offering each experience into dialog with the Creator. On one occasion, she commented that she tried to make her very breathing a thanksgiving. She spoke of the name of Jesus as an antidote to discord and recommended simply repeating "Jesus, Jesus, Jesus" as prayer (De Barberey, *Elizabeth Seton*, p. 157).

In 1816, a sudden, violent summer storm interrupted a remarkably peaceful night. Oddly, the moon remained visible during the storm. Elizabeth described what happened in a letter to her sister, Mary Post:

> Dropping asleep with my crucifix under my pillow and the Blessed Virgin's picture pressed on the heart, Kit and Rebecca [her daughters] fast asleep near me—think of the contrast, to wake with the sharpest lightnings and loudest thunder. . . . Every part of the house seemed struck in an instant. . . .
>
> O my Mary! How tight I held my little picture as a mark of confidence in her prayers who must be tenderly interested for souls so dearly purchased by her Son, and the crucifix held up as a silent prayer. . . .
>
> I crept away to the choir window, to see what had become of my little, peaceable Queen [the moon], who was wrapped in clouds alternately lightened as they passed over her . . . while she was tak[ing] her quiet course above them. . . .
>
> There again I found the soul which fastens on God. Storms or whirlwinds pass by or over it, but cannot stop it one moment. (Dirvin, *Mrs. Seton*, pp. 373–374)

Pause: Ask yourself: Do I use all of my experiences as subjects of my conversation with God?

Elizabeth's Words

We must pray literally without ceasing—without ceasing; in every occurrence and employment of our lives. You know I mean that prayer of the heart which is independent of place or situation, or which is, rather, a habit of lifting up the heart to God, as in a constant communication with Him. (Dirvin, *Mrs. Seton*, pp. 181–182)

As Mother Seton's strength ebbed away, stolen by tuberculosis, she still burned with desire to do more. Reacting to the effective ministry of Fathers Cooper and Bruté in Emmitsburg, she expressed her discontent in a letter to Bruté, but also acknowledged her call to prayer and simply waiting for God:

And pray, Mde. Bête, say you, why does not your zeal make its flame through your own little hemisphere? True,—but rules, prudence, subjections, opinions etc. dreadful walls to a soul wild as mine and somebodys— for me I am like a fiery horse I had when a girl which they tried to break by making him drag a heavy cart, and the poor beast was so humbled that he could never more be inspired by whips or caresses and wasted to a skeleton until he died. But you and Mr. Cooper might waste to skeletons to some purpose, and after wasting be sent still to the glories of the Kingdom. In the meantime, that Kingdom come. Every day I ask my bête soul what I do for it in my little part assigned, and can see nothing but to smile, caress, be patient, write, pray and WAIT, before Him. (Annabelle M. Melville, *Elizabeth Bayley Seton*, pp. 284–285)

For Elizabeth, prayer set her sights on God. She described the effects of focusing on God in this way:

Coral, in the ocean, is a strip of pale green. Remove it from its native bed, it becomes firm, does not bend, and is almost like a rock. Its tender color is changed to a bright vermilion; so it is with us, submerged in the ocean of this world, subject to the vicissitudes of its waves, ready to yield under the force of each wave of temptation.

But as soon as our soul elevates itself, and as soon as it sighs for heaven, the pale green of our feeble hope is transformed into the pure vermilion of this divine and constant love. There we look upon the overthrow of nature and the fall of empires with unshakeable constancy and confidence. (De Barberey, *Elizabeth Seton*, p. 97)

Reflection

Jesus advised us to pray always. On the face of it, this seems impossible. Even if we could find the time and a quiet space, our problems and preoccupations, imaginations and thoughts, would likely run wild, scattering any talk with God.

As a wife and mother, and later as a teacher, administrator, and religious superior, Mother Seton must have sometimes felt beset by problems and preoccupations. Her comments about prayer indicate how she prayed always. First, she used her experiences as the content of her prayer. Rather than setting them aside, she brought everything to God. Next, she prayed simply by repeating the name of Jesus; no fancy formulas or complicated prayers were necessary. Sometimes, when Elizabeth could not do everything that she desired to do for God and humankind, her prayer consisted of simply waiting on God, being attentive to creation and the Creator. In these plain ways, Elizabeth Seton prayed without ceasing.

✧ If the weather permits, take a walk alone. Observe the world of nature about you. Walk slowly, drinking in the sights, smells, and sounds all around you. At some point, focus on one object—a leaf, a whole tree, a flower, a snow-covered fence. Gaze at this object as if it were the most precious in the universe. You may want to touch and even smell the object. When you feel ready, invite Jesus into the scene with you. Tell him what is in your heart.

✧ If you cannot go outside, relax as totally as possible. Stretch all your muscles from foot to head. Then breathe deeply and slowly for a few minutes. After closing your eyes, invite your imagination to lead you to a favorite spot in nature: a shoreline, a clearing in the woods, your vegetable garden, anywhere. See, smell, and hear everything in the scene. Be attentive. Focus your attention on individual objects, savoring the sensations. Invite Jesus to a place at your side in this spot of beauty, and open your heart to him.

✧ Attend to God present. Sit quietly. Breathe deeply. Relax. When you feel calm, pray Jesus' name with every intake and exhalation of your breath. Like Elizabeth, simply pray "Jesus, Jesus."

If you wish to cease praying the sacred name, do so. Just sit, quietly attentive to God present. If worries flood in, begin reciting Jesus' name again.

✧ In God's presence, review your day. Let images of the day flow through your mind like film through a motion picture camera. Occasionally you may want to freeze an image and talk with Jesus about the situation, personal relationship, or concern. Ask Jesus what he thinks about it. Pray your experience, bringing Jesus into areas of concern. When your film comes to an end, offer Jesus thanks, praise, and any petitions. Close with the Lord's Prayer.

✧ Today, and perhaps for the next few days, each time you enter a room, get into your car, or start a new activity, say "I remember that you, God, are here with me." Evaluate your experience with this question: In what practical ways can I recall God's presence each and every day?

✧ Sing, hum, or whistle a favorite hymn in praise and thanks to God. If you find singing an enjoyable way of praying, consider how you could make music part of your way of prayer.

God's Word

Always be joyful; pray constantly; and for all things give thanks; this is the will of God for you in Christ Jesus. (1 Thessalonians 5:16–18)

Any one of you who is in trouble should pray; anyone in good spirits should sing a psalm. . . . Pray for one another to be cured; the heartfelt prayer of someone upright works very powerfully. (James 5:13–16)

Closing prayer: May I always be joyful and pray constantly. Thank you, gracious God, for the closeness of your spirit and for urging my heart to fervent, unending prayer.

✧ Meditation 6 ✧

Christ's Presence in the Eucharist

Theme: The presence of Christ in the Eucharist drew Elizabeth like a magnet and fulfilled her lifelong yearning for closeness with him.

Opening prayer: "Adored Lord, increase my faith, perfect it, crown it; Thine own, Thy choicest, dearest gift. Having drawn me from the pit, and drawn me to Thy fold, keep me in Thy sweet pastures and lead me to eternal life" (De Barberey, *Elizabeth Seton*, p. 156).

About Elizabeth

Elizabeth became a devoted Christian early in life and actively participated in her Episcopal congregation. Elizabeth's friends and relatives were members of this church, and Elizabeth counted the curate of Trinity Church, Reverend John Henry Hobart, among her friends.

At that time, the Catholic community in the United States was tiny, poor, composed mainly of immigrants, and alien to the world in which Elizabeth moved. Catholic practices seemed strange and rather suspect. In all likelihood, Elizabeth would have remained an Episcopalian all her life except for two circumstances: first, her trip to Italy and her attachment to the devout Catholic Filicchi family; and second, the centrality of the Eucharist in Catholic worship. During her lifetime, belief in Christ's real presence in the Eucharist varied greatly among individual Episcopalians and among Episcopal congregations, and for them, the Eucharist did not play as central a role in worship as it did among Catholics.

At Mass in Italy with the Filicchis, Elizabeth was truly shocked when a British tourist remarked in a stage whisper, "This is what they call their *Real Presence*." She responded in her journal: "My very heart trembled with shame and sorrow for his unfeeling interruption of their sacred adoration. . . . Involuntarily I . . . thought secretly on the word of St. Paul, with starting tears, 'They discern not the Lord's Body'" (Dirvin, *Mrs. Seton*, p. 136).

Toward the end of her stay with the Filicchis, Elizabeth revealed to her confidant, Rebecca Seton:

> How happy would we be, if we believed what these dear souls believe: that they *possess God* in the Sacrament, and that He remains in their churches and is carried to them when they are sick! Oh, my! when they carry the Blessed Sacrament under my window, while I feel the full loneliness and sadness of my case, I cannot stop the tears at the thought: My God! how happy would I be, even so far away from all so dear, if I could find You in the church as they do. . . . (Dirvin, *Mrs. Seton*, p. 137)

When Elizabeth returned to America, she was in a state of confusion. She asked Antonio Filicchi, who had escorted her on the voyage, to instruct her in Catholicism. He responded conscientiously.

During the next weeks, Elizabeth prayed and pondered about turning to the Catholic church. She realized that opposition to such a change would be strong and hostile. One Sunday she went to Saint Paul's Episcopal Church. She later wrote: "I got in a side pew which turned my face towards the Catholic Church in the next street, and found myself twenty times speaking to the Blessed Sacrament *there*, instead of looking at the naked altar where I was, or minding the routine of prayers" (Dirvin, *Mrs. Seton*, p. 154).

Her belief in the real presence of Christ in the Eucharist proved to be a major force in drawing Elizabeth to Catholicism. On 25 March 1805, she made her first communion as a Catholic. In great joy, she wrote Amabilia Filicchi: "At last, Amabilia, at last, GOD IS MINE AND I AM HIS! Now, let all go its round—*I Have Received Him*" (Dirvin, *Mrs. Seton*, p. 168).

Pause: Reflect on this question: What is the state of my own belief in the real presence of Jesus in the Eucharist?

Elizabeth's Words

Jesus then is *there* we can go, receive Him, *he is our own—* were we to pause and think of this thro' Eternity . . . that *he is There* (oh heavenly theme!) is as certainly true as that Bread naturally taken removes my hunger—so this Bread of Angels removes my pain, my cares, warms, cheers, sooths, contents and renews my whole being. (Kelly and Melville, *Selected Writings*, p. 70)

Reflection

Elizabeth's longing for the actual reception of Jesus in the Eucharist was so strong that a Sunday without Holy Communion, both as an Episcopalian and after she became a Catholic, was truly sorrowful. The eucharistic processions and Masses in Italy thrilled her. Joy swept through her when she received Christ for the first time. Mother Seton believed literally in Jesus' words: "'This is my body given for you; do this in remembrance of me. . . . This cup is the new covenant in my blood poured out for you'" (Luke 22:19–20). The Eucharist consoled her, strengthened her, and gave her quiet and sustained joy.

✧ Meditate on the section "Elizabeth's Words." Read the passage aloud, savoring words or phrases that seem especially meaningful. Then pose these questions to yourself for reflection or journaling:

✦ How strongly do I believe that Jesus is present in the Eucharist?

✦ Are there any obstacles to my belief in Christ's real presence in the Eucharist?

✦ Can I recall times when Holy Communion soothed, calmed, or warmed me?

✧ Recall your first communion: the preparation, the studies, the interest of your family, the attitude of your friends, and the actual event. Who was there? How did you feel before and after? Has your life been different since that first communion?

✧ The Eucharist is called Holy Communion because it unites us with the people of God. Receiving communion commits us to service to all God's people. Picture those persons, both living and dead, whom you love most, and gather them together in your mind. Recall the sick, the suffering, and the poor people who are also people of God. How do you express your solidarity with and service to God's people? Pray for your loved ones and for God's poor, suffering, and sick people.

✧ Slowly and repeatedly pray, "God is mine, and I am God's."

✧ Imagine that you are writing a letter to Elizabeth about the passage from 1 Corinthians 11:23–26 in the following "God's Word." After meditating on the passage, write your reflections to her.

God's Word

For the tradition I received from the Lord and also handed on to you is that on the night he was betrayed, the Lord Jesus took some bread, and after he had given thanks, he broke it, and he said, "This is my body, which is for you; do this in remembrance of me." And in the same way, with the cup after supper, saying, "This cup is the new covenant in my blood. Whenever you drink it, do this as a memorial of me." Whenever you eat this bread, then, and drink this cup, you are proclaiming the Lord's death until he comes. (1 Corinthians 11:23–26)

Closing prayer: Bread of Life, I give you praise and thanks for the priceless gift of yourself. May I always receive your body and blood with trust and hope, and may communion unite me with all your people, especially your poor and helpless ones.

Not My Will but Yours

Theme: Elizabeth believed that every event and circumstance expressed God's will in some way. Her happiness rested in the thought that everything ultimately happens for the best.

Opening prayer: I pray for the grace to prefer God's will to my own.

About Elizabeth

Around the time Elizabeth's third child was due, Will's father died, leaving Elizabeth and her husband to take on the care of Will's six brothers and sisters. To add to their troubles, his father's business had been going from bad to worse. Will struggled to keep the shipping business afloat, but the firm failed. Soon Will and Elizabeth found creditors hounding them; in short order, they were bankrupt. Exacerbated by strain and worry, Will grew weaker as the tuberculosis took a stronger hold.

By 1802, Elizabeth acknowledged that Will had little time to live. In hopes of prolonging his life, they sailed to Italy. Indeed by the end of the seven-week voyage, Will seemed better. However, the happiness of reaching land ended when they were quarantined in a lazaretto. Because their ship had come from New York, where a yellow fever epidemic rampaged, the Italian authorities were suspicious of Will's illness. The damp conditions in their stone cell cancelled any beneficial effects of the voyage. After twenty-six days in quarantine, Elizabeth wrote:

> The dampness about us would be thought dangerous for a person in health—and my William's sufferings—oh! well I know that God is *above, Capitano* [director of the quarantine], you need not always point your silent look and finger there; if I thought our condition the providence of *man*, instead of the *"weeping Magdalen"*—as you so graciously call me—you would find me a lioness, willing to burn your *lazaretto* about your ears, if it was possible, that I might carry off my poor prisoner to breathe the air of heaven in some more seasonable place. To keep a poor soul who comes to your country for his life, thirty days shut up in damp walls, smoke and wind from all corners . . . and now the shadow of death, trembling if he only stands a few minutes! He is to go to Pisa for his health— this day his prospects are very far from Pisa—but oh, my heavenly Father! I know that these contradictory events are permitted and guided by Thy Wisdom, which only is *light*. (Dirvin, *Mrs. Seton*, pp. 122–123)

A few days following the family's release from quarantine, Will Seton died. Elizabeth concluded, "His soul was released—and mine from a struggle next to death" (Dirvin, *Mrs. Seton*, p.125).

Not only did Elizabeth believe that God's wisdom guides all events but she also trusted that God's will could be manifested through wise and loving friends. Elizabeth placed particularly strong faith in the Filicchis. They had, she believed, been God's instruments in drawing her into the Catholic church. Thus, when she considered the work she was beginning in Baltimore, she wrote to them:

> The subject of my last [letter] to you . . . so nearly concerns all my hopes and expectations for this world, which is to do something—if ever so little—towards promoting our dear and holy Faith that I am sure you would give me

some encouragement, if you had any opportunity; or your reasons for not encouraging our plan (if indeed it is the Will of God that it shall not be realized). It has long since been committed to Him; but I cannot help begging always in Communion while my heart is turned toward Livorno: "Oh, dear Lord, put in their hearts whatever is your Holy Will for me." (Dirvin, *Mrs. Seton*, p. 226)

Elizabeth sought to know and do God's will in all matters. Doing God's will was often her only consolation.

Pause: Ponder this question: How do you discern what is God's will and what is your own?

Elizabeth's Words

What was the first rule of our dear Savior's life? You know it was to do His Father's Will. Well, then, the first end I propose in our daily work is to do the Will of God; secondly, to do it in the manner He Wills It; and thirdly, to do it because it is His Will.

I know what His Will is by those who direct me; whatever they bid me do, if it is ever so small in itself, is the Will of God for me. Then do it in the manner He wills it—not sewing an old thing as if it was new, or a new thing as if it was old; not fretting because the oven is too hot, or in a fuss because it is too cold. You understand—not flying and driving because you are hurried, nor creeping like a snail because no one pushes you. Our dear Savior was never in extremes.

The third object is to do this *Will* because God wills it, that is, to be ready to quit at any moment, and to do anything else we may be called to. (Dirvin, *Mrs. Seton*, p. 340)

Reflection

Elizabeth's faith was her rock of strength, and her desire to do God's will, her light. Though such steadfastness and calm in adversity may seem hard to believe, her journals and letters provide ample evidence that she suffered deeply. In one of her letters to Julia Scott, she wrote of how she had been struggling to maintain a joyful demeanor while taking care of all the young Setons and fighting the opposition to her interest in becoming a Catholic. She concluded, "The smile of content . . . often conceals the sharp thorn in the heart" (Code, *Letters*, p. 124). Like all of us, Elizabeth sometimes suffered doubts. These too are described in her journals.

Nevertheless, Elizabeth relied on God's providence and actively sought to know and then do God's will. In her many writings, she did not claim to have direct revelations from heaven as to what God wanted her to do. Instead, she pondered her experience, studied the Scriptures, prayed for light, and beseeched the good counsel of her friends and advisers. In the end, God's will became manifest to her.

✧ Read the section "Elizabeth's Words" slowly several times. Then reflect on these questions:
✦ How do I do God's will in my daily work?
✦ Do I do my daily work in the manner God wills?
✦ Do I do my daily work because it is God's will?

✧ In your journal or on other paper, construct a time line of your life, marking the significant moments and changes of direction: for example, a marriage, a vow, the death of a parent, a move or event that affected you deeply. Choose one of these events and ponder the way in which your life changed, or how it would have been different if this happening had not taken place. As you look back, ask yourself how you see the hand of God shaping your life and how the loving providence of God has brought good out of something that might have seemed tragic at the time.

✧ In discerning God's will, Elizabeth seemed to follow a process something like the one described here. Use this process to consider what is God's will about some key issue or decision you face. Focus on one problem or decision.
✦ What do the Scriptures tell you about this situation or deci-

sion? Search the Gospels and the Epistles for the advice Jesus would give you.

✦ In prayer, talk with the Holy Spirit about the situation or decision. Discuss every aspect.

✦ Seek the counsel of someone you trust and who can help you.

✦ Speak once more to the Holy Spirit. Pray repeatedly these words of Jesus: "'Let your will be done, not mine'" (Luke 22:42). Then listen with an open heart, mind, and will.

✦ Decide, act, and evaluate the results, acknowledging that God will help you each step of the way.

God's Word

Give in to God, then; resist the devil, and [the devil] will run away from you. The nearer you go to God, the nearer God will come to you. (James 4:7–8)

Closing prayer: At the start of each day, may I willingly say: God's will, nothing more, nothing less, nothing else.

✧ **Meditation 8** ✧

Following the Demands of Love

Theme: Partings punctuated Elizabeth's life. Though she grieved along the way, she trusted that each parting was God's will and would lead to greater love.

Opening prayer: God of all consolation, help me to respond fully to your call even if it means parting from what is familiar, safe, or comfortable.

About Elizabeth

Elizabeth's basic orientation inclined her toward a willing resignation to God's loving disposition of her life. Whenever choices had to be made, the Divine Will became the focus of Elizabeth's deliberations. Nonetheless, even when she was convinced that God called her to new love, each parting tore at her heart.

Though Elizabeth journeyed to Italy in hopes that the trip would help her husband, Will, the decision to go tore Elizabeth's heart. She could not allow her husband—ill and in danger of death—to travel alone, but going on the voyage meant leaving four of her young children, the baby still under a year old and needing to be weaned before the mother could depart.

Elizabeth and Will took their oldest child, Anna, with them, leaving the others in the care of Eliza Sadler, a lifelong friend. In those days it was quite common for children to be kept by relatives or friends, but even so, Elizabeth begged Eliza, "Take my darlings often in your arms!" (Dirvin, *Mrs. Seton*, p. 111).

After Will's death and during her grieving, God called Elizabeth to new ways of loving, ways she could never have imagined and ways that demanded more partings. Elizabeth felt called to Catholicism even though this meant severing ties with the Episcopal community that included her family and close friends. She procrastinated partly because she lacked surety, partly because she loved the Episcopal congregation in which she had been raised, and partly because the only Catholic church in her neighborhood was a spiritual home to poor immigrants and described by her social peers as "a horrid place of spits and pushing" (Dirvin, *Mrs. Seton*, p. 171). Nevertheless, Elizabeth parted from the Episcopal communion because she became convinced that God was inviting her to a new life.

Elizabeth lost some of her friends and incurred the wrath of those who saw the Catholic church as an enemy. The widowed Elizabeth found eking out a living for herself and her children to be an almost insurmountable challenge. The little school she started soon came to naught, partly because of the opposition of her former friends and new enemies. But God used this failure as the occasion to call her to her next challenge.

Elizabeth described her difficult economic situation to Father William Dubourg. He wanted to establish a Catholic school in Baltimore and quickly concluded that Elizabeth would be the ideal person to direct his school. After negotiations and arrangements, Elizabeth again faced leave-taking: from New York, from her friends and family, from all she had known. As she said to a friend, "Can a heart swell so high and not burst? . . . the dear, dear, dear adored Will [of God] . . . may it control, regulate and perfect us; and when all is over, how we will rejoice that it was done!" (Dirvin, *Mrs. Seton*, p. 210). Elizabeth moved to Baltimore and, soon after, Emmitsburg, following what she discerned to be God's will.

In Emmitsburg, Elizabeth found herself the head of a growing community of religious women with a boarding school for girls as the principal work of the community. She wrote to her friend Catherine Dupleix: "Your poor little ship-wrecked friend is finishing her career under the strange and ill-placed title of abbess of a convent. . . . It is hard to live so far from the first ties of my life, but, as you know, circumstances sometimes made a residence among them rather painful" (Kelly, *Numerous Choirs*, p. 141). So Mrs. Seton gradually became Mother Seton, leaving the relatively clear role she had as mother and teacher and adding a new role and set of responsibilities. She did not hesitate, however, telling another friend: "The hand that allots always proportions; that we well know" (Code, *Letters*, p. 253).

On her deathbed, Elizabeth gracefully prepared for her last departure. Even though parting from the sisters, friends, two sons, and her daughter, Kit, would be painful, she looked forward to union with God, Will, her family, and friends. With so many partings in her life, Elizabeth had come to know that leaving loved ones would always lead to encounters with new loved ones and reunions with those who had already departed. After all, her previous partings had faithfully led her deeper into the arms of God, who is love.

Pause: Ponder some of your partings. Have they led you to greater wisdom and love?

Elizabeth's Words

As she was discerning her future, especially the possibility of leaving New York, Elizabeth wrote Antonio Filicchi:

> I repeat to you, Antonio . . . these are my happiest days. Sometimes the harassed mind, wearied with continual contradiction to all it would most covet—solitude! silence! peace!—sighs for a change; but five minutes' recollection procures an immediate act of resignation, convinced that this is the day of salvation for me. And if, like a coward, I should run away from the field of battle, I am sure

the very peace I seek would fly from me, and the state of penance sanctified by the Will of God would be again wished for as the safest and surest road. (Dirvin, *Mrs. Seton*, p. 207)

Doing God's will brought Elizabeth surety and solace, but so did knowing that God dwelled within her no matter where her partings led:

He dwells within—our soul his palace! . . . Converse with him is without bounds or limits—as often as we will enter within ourselves, and as long a time as we will remain, we may enjoy this heavenly commerce in perfect liberty—

Many seek to love God by different methods but there is none so short and so easy as *to do everything for his love*, to set this seal on all our actions. . . .

Good Will, Simplicity, and Confidence, are the Keys of the Sanctuary of *DIVINE LOVE*. (Kelly and Melville, *Selected Writings*, p. 357)

Reflection

Parting can come in many forms: the death of a friend, moving to a new town, breaking off a relationship, giving away a favorite pet, or even selling a trusty old car. No matter what the parting, it is seldom easy. Even when we know that growing things must change or shrivel and die, the actual cost of separation is difficult. Even a rut can become comfortable after a while.

Elizabeth understood this, but she knew why she was choosing the path she did: to do the will of God, which is to love. Her writings reveal her very human anxiety about the partings, but she was able to keep her final goal in mind, making it possible to let go of a present love for a greater love. The God who dwells inside her and us sustains, comforts, and draws her and us forward.

✧ Recall and list the significant partings in your life. Remember the reasons for each parting, who was involved, and

what you felt at the time. Then reflect on the effects of each parting and, perhaps in writing, ponder these questions:
+ What opportunities for new life did this parting open for me?
+ Did any resentments and hurt block out the positive aspects of this parting?
+ Looking back, to what was God inviting me by this move?
+ How is my life different because of this leave-taking?

Thank God for the positive outcomes of each parting. Ask God for understanding about moves that still seem negative.

✧ If you are in the midst of making a decision about some parting—whether from a job, a relationship, or some other leave-taking—try these steps in your discernment:
+ Pray to the Holy Spirit for guidance.
+ Consult with friends or associates who know you well and who have a sense of God's will for human beings.
+ Read the Scriptures, especially passages related to your decision.
+ Listen to your heart when you ask: Will this move bring new life, new possibilities to love? What are my hopes and goals for such a move?
+ Pray again, beseeching the Holy Spirit's wisdom and strength.

✧ Elizabeth consoled herself in times of parting by remembering that God's will was most important and that God dwelled within her no matter where she went. Repeatedly pray this adaptation of Elizabeth's words: "My soul is God's palace!" In the future, when you are separated from loved ones or in the midst of parting, offer this prayer to recall the companionship of your Holy Friend.

✧ Another sort of leave-taking consists of parting company with old habits. Write a list of habits that you would like to walk away from. Pick one that is particularly troublesome to you. Then picture Jesus, your habit, and yourself sitting in your living room. You have met to discuss a divorce between yourself and your old habit. Jesus, as arbiter, poses the following questions. Listen to what the old habit has to say, then respond.

Jesus asks:

✦ Why do you have such a strong hold on our friend here?
✦ How did this whole thing get started?
✦ Do you think that . . . would be better off without you? How so?
✦ What is . . . going to have to do to part company with you?

When your unwelcome habit and you have finished answering Jesus' questions, continue the dialog. Ask Jesus for his advice about the situation.

Now ponder what you really wish to do, especially if the old habit is preventing you from loving God and your neighbor more fully. Call on God for the grace to cope with this desired change.

God's Word

Then Peter answered and said, "Look, we have left everything and followed you. What are we to have, then?" Jesus said to them, "In truth I tell you, when everything is made new again and the Son of Man is seated on his throne of glory, you yourselves will sit on twelve thrones to judge the twelve tribes of Israel. And everyone who has left houses, brothers, sisters, father, mother, children or land for the sake of my name will receive a hundred times as much, and also inherit eternal life." (Matthew 19:27–29)

Closing prayer: As I look to you, God, as my greater love, may I be confident in your loving direction, and may I know that you are always with me.

Loving Service

Theme: Compassionate service to family and to people in need is as integral to Elizabeth's spirituality as it is to Christian spirituality.

Opening prayer: Good Shepherd, may I serve your people with compassion and wisdom.

About Elizabeth

Elizabeth's father, Dr. Richard Bayley, served as physician and director of the Staten Island Quarantine Station for immigrants coming into New York harbor from all over the world. During one summer, Elizabeth and the children went to stay with Dr. Bayley on the island. Each day the flood of sick and pathetic immigrants seemed to increase, and yellow fever took many lives. Wracked by the desire to help, Elizabeth wrote:

> Rebecca, I cannot sleep. The dying and the dead possess my mind. Babies perishing at the empty breast of the expiring mother. And this is not fancy, but the scene that surrounds me. Father says such was never known before, that there is actually twelve children that must die for mere want of sustenance, unable to take *more* than the breast and, from the wretchedness of their parents, deprived of it, as they have lain ill for many days in the ship

without food, air or *changing. Merciful Father!* Oh, how readily would I give them each a turn of Kit's [her infant daughter's] treasure if in my choice! (Dirvin, *Mrs. Seton,* p. 91)

Elizabeth's desire to serve poor people did find active expression, however. While Will, her husband, tried to keep his failing business going, Elizabeth took care of her own family, fed and looked after Will's six brothers and sisters, taught school to all the children, and visited sick and poor families. She described one of her typical days:

I have cut out my two suits today and partly made one. Heard all the lessons, too, and had a two hours' visit from my widow Veley—no work, no wood, child sick, etc.— and should I complain, with a bright fire within, bright, bright moon over my shoulder, and the darlings all well, hallooing and dancing?—I have played for them this half hour. (Dirvin, *Mrs. Seton,* p. 102)

Elizabeth joined with a number of prominent New York women to form a benevolent association, The Society for the Relief of Widows with Small Children. Elizabeth was treasurer of the society until 1805 and, along with the others, raised funds for relief, visited needy people, and provided them with food and clothing made by the members. Elizabeth even petitioned New York authorities to allow the society to raise needed funds by lottery.

Founding the Sisters of Charity at Emmitsburg was a logical outgrowth of Elizabeth's compassion and experience of service. In a letter of 1810, she included this account of the community's service:

We are now twelve, and as many again are waiting for admission. I have a very very large school to superintend every day, and the entire charge of the religious instruction of all the country round. All happy to the Sisters of Charity who are night and day devoted to the sick and ignorant. Our blessed Bishop intends removing a detachment of us to Baltimore to perform the same duties there. (Kelly and Melville, *Selected Writings,* p. 279)

Until she died, Mother Seton continued to compassionately serve her family, the sisters, and the many needy people who came to her. In addition to the foundations in Emmitsburg and Baltimore, the Sisters of Charity opened other orphanages and schools to serve the growing number of Catholic immigrants surging into the country.

Near the end of her life, she told Antonio Filicchi: "Our poor little *mustard seed* spreads its branches very well, they have written us from New York to come and take 8 hundred children of the state school besides our orphan asylum" (Kelly and Melville, *Selected Writings*, p. 291).

Pause: How are you serving God's people?

Elizabeth's Words

Mother Seton gave these instructions to the sisters:

> So our bodies, as Sisters of Charity must be neither spared
> or looked at, no labours or sufferings considered for a mo-
> ment but rather only asking what is this for my God! see-
> ing everything only in that one view *our God* and *our
> Eternity.* . . .
>
> This is my commandment that ye love one another as
> I have loved you—
>
> The charity of our blessed lord in the course of his
> ministry had [these] distinct qualities which should be the
> model of our conduct. it was gentle Benevolent and uni-
> versal. (Kelly and Melville, *Selected Writings,* p. 325)

Reflection

In Elizabeth Seton's spirituality, indeed in Christian spirituality, compassionate service is integral. Jesus fed, healed, listened
to, challenged, and embraced his friends and enemies. Elizabeth did likewise, and the little "mustard seed" spread.

Although she founded a community of women to serve
as Sisters of Charity, Mother Seton had long before been a sister
of charity. Jesus calls all of his followers to be sisters and brothers of charity.

Many valiant Christian persons serve others, albeit quietly and simply. They are the people we turn to in trouble, the
ones who are first at our door with a casserole in times of sickness. They offer a ride to church in stormy weather; they bring
a bouquet of tulips from the spring garden or peaches from
the tree in the yard. The role of service to others need not be
noticeable to be effective.

Some valiant Christians volunteer segments of their lives
to give of their skills in other lands: healing, teaching, preach-
ing, and farming. In turn, the lives of those they serve reflect
the Gospel to the volunteers. Even so, whatever the fashion,
loving service makes Jesus' love manifest in a world desperate
for that love. Elizabeth knew this and lived it.

✧ Review the sections "About Elizabeth" and "Elizabeth's Words." Then reflect on this question: How am I serving my sisters and brothers right now, even if only in simple and quiet ways?

✧ When was the last time you received an unwelcome phone call? Perhaps it was a friend who wanted to talk and you were busy, or an acquaintance who needed help or advice? In what spirit did you receive this call to service?

✧ Many of us have seen people on a corner, holding a sign, "Want Work for Food." Write your reflections on these questions:
✦ Do I allow myself to really see these people?
✦ How does such a sight make me feel?
✦ What could I do?
✦ What do I do?
✦ Is there some systemic change that I could help bring about in society that would even slightly rectify the forces that cause men and women to be in such situations?

✧ Time is a precious commodity and a valuable gift. Meditate on these questions:
✦ Who gives me their time and makes me feel valuable with this gift?
✦ Who deserves the gift of my time?
✦ Do I give this gift generously and regularly?
✦ What can I do to make this gift more available to people who need it?

✧ Service to our neighbor should be a free gift. Meditate on and then respond to each statement:
✦ I gave the gift of healing (physical, emotional, or spiritual) to . . . when I . . .
✦ I gave the gift of feeding to . . . when I . . .
✦ I gave the gift of sheltering to . . . when I . . .
✦ I gave the gift of hospitality to . . . when I . . .
✦ I gave the gift of visiting . . . when I . . .
Now thank God for the opportunities to give service that you have had. Pray for each person brought to mind.

✧ Visit a shut-in or someone who is sick. Call someone who is grieving or lonely. Contribute to a food bank, a homeless shelter, or some other charitable agency. These are action prayers.

God's Word

If one of the brothers or one of the sisters is in need of clothes and has not enough food to live on, and one of you says to them, "I wish you well; keep yourself warm and eat plenty," without giving them these bare necessities of life, then what good is that? In the same way faith: if good deeds do not go with it, it is quite dead. (James 2:15–17)

Closing prayer: Jesus, servant to all humankind, give me the vision and the humility to see you in other people, especially in those who are poor and suffering. Grant me the courage and compassion to be your hands, your wisdom, and your heart in service to my sisters and brothers.

Forgiving
and Unselfish Love

Theme: Elizabeth sought to show the face of Jesus to all persons regardless of their response to her.

Opening prayer: God, with unselfish love, let me be open and available to everyone, and may I be forgiving to those who cause me pain and suffering.

About Elizabeth

As the news spread that Elizabeth was becoming a Catholic, relatives, friends, and associates turned on her with bitter invectives and dire predictions. Despite the pain at such rejection, Elizabeth reacted with forgiveness and charity. The love she bore her critics and her supporters did not depend on a loving response from them. Rooted in her belief in God's love, Elizabeth strove to look for the good in each situation and every person.

Pondering the troubles during her period of conversion, Elizabeth wrote to her friend Julia Scott:

> You asked me long ago about my religious principles. I am gently, quietly and silently a good Catholic. The rubs, etc., are all past. No one appears to know it except by

showing redoubled kindness—*only* a few knotty hearts that must talk of something, and the worse they say is: "So much trouble has turned her brain." Well, I kiss my crucifix, which I have loved for so many years, and say they are only mistaken.

So we go, dear Julia, traveling on. Take care, Miss, where you stop. (Dirvin, *Mrs. Seton*, p. 187)

Such unselfish and forgiving love did not always come easily; sometimes Elizabeth had to grit her teeth and steel herself. In a letter to Filippo Filicchi, she revealed the effort she expended in being charitable:

My daily object is to keep close to your first advice (with St. Francis) to take every event gently and quietly, and oppose good nature and cheerfulness to every contradiction; which succeeds so well that now it is an acknowledged opinion that Mrs. William Seton is in a very happy situation; and Mr. Wilkes says, speaking of *his* possessions: "Yet Providence does not do so much for me as for you, as it makes you happy and contented in every situation." Yet indeed—for how can he build who has not the rock for his foundation? But Mrs. William Seton is obliged to watch every moment to keep up the reality of this appearance. You know, Filicchi, what it costs to be always humble and satisfied. (Dirvin, *Mrs. Seton*, p. 205)

Elizabeth recognized and rejoiced in the many blessings God sent her way. The foundation of her strength, forgiveness, and charity was God, the rock.

As leader of the fledgling religious community, Elizabeth tried to show this same forgiveness and charity to the sisters. She described her attitude:

I am as a mother surrounded by numerous offspring; their dispositions are different; they are not all equally lovable, nor conform to all that pleases me, but the mother is bound to love them all, to instruct them and to provide for their happiness; to furnish an example of cheerfulness and peace and resignation, considering each one in particular, and not according to the grades of merit or demerit, but as proceeding from the same source, and tending to the same end. (De Barberey, *Elizabeth Seton*, p. 333)

Pause: Do you find it difficult to forgive insults and to love without counting the cost?

Elizabeth's Words

How many rebukes and contradictions did [Jesus] endure without complaining—his apostles without learning education or intelligence, often unable to comprehend his instructions obliging him to repeat and reexplain the same things—often requiring his mediation in their dissentions living with them and conversing with them and so far from appearing to be troubled with their presence he always desired to have them with him.

Thus he might well say to us, "come learn of me for I am meek and lowly of heart" and at the same time know how much you ought to be so—and have I been as my blessed Lord have I learned to bear the weaknesses of others, they are obliged to bear with mine, and is it now very reasonable that I should require from them indulgence for the many faults that escape me and yet be unwilling to allow any to them—the bad qualities of others should perfect and purify my Charity rather than weaken it, for if I should only *have* charity for those who are faultless, it will be intirely without merit, or rather it would not be any at all as there are no persons without faults. and if I had to live only with angels this mild and gentle conduct would be of no use as it would not be required. (Kelly and Melville, *Selected Writings*, pp. 325–326)

Reflection

Jesus invites us to a life of forgiving, unselfish love that cares for the welfare of other people even when love is unrequited. Christlike love fosters the best good of other people in their concrete situations. Often this kind of love requires patience, tolerance, firmness of purpose, and selflessness: a big heart and a generous spirit.

Elizabeth's forgiving, unselfish love was often sorely test-
ed by both friends and enemies. So she prayed, studied the
word of God, and relied on God's grace. Calmness, integrity,
and contentment were the fruits of her love. Thus she confounded her critics and nurtured the spirit of her community.

✧ Select the one line from "Elizabeth's Words" that most
touches or challenges you. Pray it over and over again, relish-
ing its meaning and call for you.

✧ List instances in which you have forgiven people who
have offended you and in which you have acted for the good
of other people in an unselfish way during this week; no false
modesty, please.

Thank God for these opportunities to love, remembering
that only God's grace allows us to love.

✧ Now thank God for people who have shown you forgiveness recently and people who have sacrificed themselves
for your good. Offer each name to God and then pray: "For
their forgiving, unselfish love, I thank you, God of Mercy and
Love."

✧ Recall instances when you gave of yourself, acted
charitably, and then felt ignored and unappreciated. Maybe
you sent a long letter and special card to someone at Christmas and received only a signed greeting back. Or maybe you
spent hours organizing and working at the parish potluck and
raffle, but the pastor forgot to include your name on the list of
people he thanked.

In your journal, write responses to these questions for reflection:

✦ How did I feel in each case?
✦ How did I respond?
✦ Did I find forgiveness in my heart?

If you still feel hurt or hostile about these incidents, pray
for the spirit of forgiveness and charity. In some ritualized
way, let go of your resentment or anger. For example, light a
candle and, while gazing at the flame, pray: "Spirit of Light, I

give you my hurt. Fill my soul with peace and wisdom. I let go of [name the person and the hurt] in forgiveness."

✧ Think of someone you find hard to treat charitably. Explain to God why this person is hard for you to love. Ask God for the grace to forgive the person and to care for him or her with more tolerance, patience, and kindness.

God's Word

Treat others as you would like people to treat you. If you love those who love you, what credit can you expect? Even sinners love those who love them. . . . Instead, love your enemies and do good to them, and lend without any hope of return. You will have a great reward, and you will be children of the Most High, for [God] is kind to the ungrateful and the wicked. (Luke 6:31–35)

Closing prayer: Loving God, let me willingly and openly offer my love to all you send to me, and whether or not there is a return of love, let me thank you.

✧ **Meditation 11** ✧

Friendship

Theme: Elizabeth had a gift for friendship, and her faith served to deepen her concern for her friends.

Opening prayer: Holy Friend, thank you for the gift of my friends. May you be the gift we give to each other.

About Elizabeth

When Elizabeth was in her teen years, separated from her father and living with relatives, she formed several deep friendships that lasted her whole life. These did not develop by accident; Elizabeth knew that friendship is a treasured gift that cannot be taken for granted. She gave freely of her own time, resources, advice, prayers, and affection.

Her letters to Julianna Scott from 1798 to 1820 present a unique and personal picture of Elizabeth's life and of her commitment to friendship. Julia Scott and Elizabeth moved in the same circles in New York society. When Julia's husband, Lewis Allaire Scott—onetime secretary of state of New York—died in March 1798, Elizabeth stayed with and consoled Julia, even though Elizabeth herself was expecting her third child momentarily. Elizabeth helped Julia close her house and prepare to move with her two children to Philadelphia where she would live with a sister.

The first of Elizabeth's letters to Julia is dated April 1798 and expresses some of her views on friendship. She wrote to Julia: "Nothing shall ever interrupt the course of my affection for you or prevent my expressing it whenever it is in my power. I am very anxious to hear of your arrival" (Code, *Letters*, p. 15).

She urged Julia to write, even if she had her little daughter Maria practice her penmanship by doing the writing:

> Do not fear to lessen my pleasure in hearing from you by so doing, for you know that one of the first rules of my happiness is to be satisfied with Good in whatever degree I can attain it; besides which it is very material that absence should not efface me from Maria's remembrance, as I have not yet lost the hope that my Anna may one day be as dear to her as you are to me. Difference of age after a certain period is very immaterial, and rather adds to affection by creating that kind of confidence we have in those who are at an age to judge of our particular feelings, and yet have more experience to give weight to advice. (Code, *Letters*, p. 15)

Throughout her life, Elizabeth maintained a steady correspondence with Julia. During the first few years of separation, she wrote two or three letters each month; in later years, five or six letters annually.

As Elizabeth's own religious faith deepened, she became more concerned that those she loved should also find the happiness and peace that had come with her own conversion. She wrote to Julia, her "dear, elegant slave of the world," of the need to think of eternity and to turn to God for guidance (Code, *Letters*, p. 237). At times she waxed too strongly and would apologize for her insistent moralizing. But the bond between Julia and Elizabeth was too strong to be broken by Elizabeth's fervor or Julia's differences of attitude.

Elizabeth often turned to Julia for financial help, especially during the early struggles of the community at Emmitsburg. Julia never failed her. For instance, in 1814 Elizabeth wrote to thank Julia for a donation and poured out her deepest feelings and concerns for her friend:

I repeat to you I shall truly love money by and by, since it is the only means by which I can hear from you. Dear, dear friend, could I but pay you back as I would wish, by opening to you the door of my heart and showing you what passed there in desires and love for you. My Julia dear, my dear precious, heaven-born friend, weighted and pressed down by the sickening atmosphere of your scene of pain and disappointment. . . .

Your dear Charlotte always sick, and poor brother, too! With that tenderness of affection I would still hang over them as twenty years ago. But, my Julia, so it is; and the heart can be heard only by Him who reads without words, and receiving the thousand sighs for souls so precious. . . . Well, Julia dear, trouble, trouble everywhere 'till, but we must be good first. Will you pray? Do, try to promise me that whenever you see the sun set you will lift your heart with mine, and pierce beyond His golden clouds. Do, do, Julia, my Julia! Pay me back for taking your money, and give me all I ask.

Your own friend,

E. A. Seton
(Code, *Letters*, pp. 236–237)

Elizabeth loved Julia and her many other friends mightily. She saw friendship as one of God's greatest gifts and, at its deepest, as a mutual opportunity for drawing closer to God.

Pause: Bring to mind and cherish the image of one of your true friends.

Elizabeth's Words

In her writings about friendship, Elizabeth makes it clear that friendship with God only makes human friendships more possible and more precious: "I find in proportion as my heart is more drawn towards the summit, it looks back with added tenderness to everyone I have ever loved; much more to those who have long possessed its entire and truest attachment" (Joseph B. Code, ed., *Daily Thoughts of Mother Seton*, April 4).

Elizabeth wrote this to Antonio Filicchi, one of her closest and most loyal friends:

> Jonathan loved David as his own soul, and if I was your brother, Antonio, I would never leave you for one hour. But, as it is, I try rather to turn every affection to God, well knowing that there alone their utmost exercise cannot be misapplied, and most ardent hopes can never be disappointed. (Joseph I. Dirvin, *The Soul of Elizabeth Seton*, p. 17)

Reflection

Aristotle praised friendship as the most spiritual of loves. Jesus told the Apostles that he did not consider them as servants, but as friends. Friendship is characterized by mutual caring and usually involves loyalty, support, and a shared view of the world. Friends help each other achieve what is good. Ultimately, friends help us find God because the love between friends is from God who is love.

As people change jobs and locations with more frequency, friendships become increasingly important sources of identity, support, and community. Certainly Elizabeth understood this; she poured out her soul to her friends, and they did the same to her. She relied on her friends like Julia and Antonio. In turn, they cherished the affection and care that she showed to them. Her friends and our friends give a human face to God's love. Moreover, human friends bolster our faith and hope through their life-giving love.

✧ Ponder this question: Who is my best friend? Reflect on all the qualities that first drew you together. What are the characteristics you admire most? What has bonded your friendship? Thank God for the gift of this friend and ask for the grace to be faithful and loyal. Then visit, call, or write your friend. Let your friend know how much he or she means to you.

✧ Our friendships usually have a basis in one particular way of presence with each other. Some people are recreational friends; that is, they began their friendship by jogging or walking together. Others became friends while attending Bread for the World gatherings; they are "common cause" friends. Beside each of the following types of friendship, list the people with whom you share this relationship. Remember that some people may be listed next to several types.

Who are my . . .
+ intellectual friends?
+ recreational friends?
+ common cause friends?
+ emotional sharing friends?
+ spiritual friends?
+ cultural interest friends?
+ work friends?

When you have finished writing, ponder the names of the people listed. Notice names that appear more than once. Is there anyone on the list that surprises you? Finally, thank God for each friend and for the different ways that you have to make friends.

✧ Out loud, pray this remark by Jesus over and over again slowly:

You are my friends
. . . .
I call you friends,
because I have made known to you
everything I have learnt. . . .

(John 15:14–15)

Then meditate on the words. Do you accept Jesus as your friend? Remembering that friendship is mutual, how are you a friend to Jesus? Enter into a conversation with Jesus about your relationship with him.

✧ Our friends can hurt us more deeply than our enemies because they know so much more about us. If you have been hurt by a friend, recall the hurt. Pray for the one who hurt you, asking that the power and love of God heal your hurt and the relationship. If the hurt remains even though the person has moved out of your life, ask God to help you let go of the hurt.

✧ Elizabeth shared her religious convictions with her friends, even to the point of asking their forgiveness for being so fervent. Do you feel right and comfortable about sharing your religious values and spiritual experiences with anyone? If so, how has being able to share helped you? If not, do you feel a need for such a friendship, and do you have any way of making such a friend?

✧ Meditate on the section "God's Word" following. Repeat it slowly as a prayer of thanksgiving to God for your friends.

God's Word

A loyal friend is a powerful defence:
　　whoever finds one has indeed found a treasure.
A loyal friend is something beyond price,
　　there is no measuring his [her] worth.
A loyal friend is the elixir of life,
　　and those who fear [God] will find one.
Whoever fears [God] makes true friends,
　　for as a person is, so is his [her] friend too.
(Ecclesiasticus 6:14–17)

Closing prayer: Thank you, my God and my friend, for the great gifts you send me in the persons of those who call me friend. Grant that we may continue our love for one another.

✧　**Meditation 12**　✧

Mary, Mother

Theme: Elizabeth's own motherhood gave her an understanding of Mary, the mother of Jesus, and of Mary's role as guide and protector.

Opening prayer: Hail Mary, full of grace, the Lord is with you. Blessed are you among women, and blessed is the fruit of your womb, Jesus.

About Elizabeth

Elizabeth is affectionately known as Mother Seton. The name fits her well because she was not only a biological mother but a spiritual one as well. She found in Mary the image of motherhood that she did not experience in her own childhood.

As a child of barely three years, Elizabeth lost her own mother to death, and through her growing years, Elizabeth felt the absence of a mother's love. Her stepmother, the second Mrs. Bayley, was absorbed in her own growing family. Elizabeth's father involved himself with the offspring of his second marriage and withdrew the attention he had formerly shown to Elizabeth. Thus Elizabeth felt the loss of her father also.

In her lonely walks, Elizabeth often looked up "for my mother . . . in heaven" (Laverty, *Loom*, p. 98). Her own lack of mothering impressed on Elizabeth the value of motherhood.

She took fond care of her stepbrothers and stepsisters whenever she resided in her father's household.

Her own motherhood was a source of great wonder for
Elizabeth. As a result, her affection for and veneration of Mary
increased. In her letters, she frequently referred to Mary's
motherhood and her nurturing and care for the child Jesus.
Mary was a kindred spirit.

During Elizabeth's stay with the Filicchis in Italy, her interest and devotion to Mary grew. She found a prayer book be-
longing to Amabilia Filicchi and opened to the Memorare.
Earnestly, Elizabeth begged Mary to be a mother to her and
her little children. She wrote to Rebecca Seton:

> God would surely refuse nothing *to his Mother*, and that
> she could not help loving and pitying the poor souls he
> died for, that I felt really I had a Mother which you know
> my foolish heart so often laments to have lost in early
> days . . . and at that moment it seemed as if I had found
> more than her, even in tenderness and pity of a Mother—
> so I cried myself to sleep on her heart. (Kelly and Melville,
> *Selected Writings*, p. 55)

Upon returning to New York, Elizabeth hesitated to teach
her Episcopal children the Hail Mary, though Anna urged her
to do so at evening prayers:

> Anna coaxes me when we are at our evening prayers to
> say Hail Mary and all say *oh do Ma* teach it to us, even lit-
> tle Bec tries to lisp it though she can scarcely speak, and I
> ask my Saviour why should we not say it, if anyone is in
> heaven *his Mother* must be there, are the Angels then who
> are so often represented as being so interested for us on
> earth, more compassionate or more exalted than she is—
> oh no no, Mary our Mother that cannot be, so I beg her
> with the confidence and tenderness of her child to pity us,
> and guide us to the true faith if we are not in it, and *if we
> are*, to obtain peace for my poor Soul, that I may be a good
> Mother to my poor darlings—for I know if God should
> leave me to myself after all my sins he would be justified
> . . . so I kiss her picture you gave me, and beg her to be a
> Mother to us. (Kelly and Melville, *Selected Writings*, pp.
> 160–161)

This confidence in Mary became stronger as Elizabeth raised her children and coped with all the sorrow that sometimes ensued. At the grave of her dear eldest daughter, Anna, a weeping Elizabeth turned to Mary, begging her to beseech Jesus to pity "a poor, poor mother—so uncertain of reunion" (Kelly and Melville, *Selected Writings*, p. 304).

Pause: Ponder this question: In what special way may Mary become a model for my life?

Elizabeth's Words

In her last instructions to the sisters, Elizabeth wrote:

MARY FULL OF GRACE—MOTHER of JESUS O! we love and honour our Jesus when we love and honour her . . . Mary returning our love to JESUS for us, our prayer passing through her heart with reflected love and excellence. Jesus delighting to receive our love embellished and purified through the heart of Mary, as from the heart of a friend every thing delights us. how can we honour the mysteries of our Jesus, without honouring Mary in them all. . . .

. . . Our best honour to Mary is the *imitation* of her Virtues—her life a model for all conditions of life—her poverty, humility, purity, love—*and Sufferings!*

Mary teaching patience with life—its commonest offices . . . Mary the first Sister of Charity on Earth. (Kelly and Melville, *Selected Writings*, pp. 328–329)

Reflection

Motherless herself from childhood, Elizabeth naturally turned to Mary, the mother given by Jesus to all of us. Elizabeth frequently celebrated Mary's love with the Hail Mary and the Memorare. As a result of her own devotion, Elizabeth urged her community and all who would listen to honor, learn from, and pray with Mary.

✧ Ponder the section "Elizabeth's Words" once again. Does Elizabeth's reasoning and devotion make sense to you? Does it challenge or affirm your present feeling about Mary?

✧ One of the most popular, traditional ways of praying with Mary is the rosary. If you pray the rosary frequently, ask yourself what it has meant to you. If you do not pray the rosary, reflect on its value as a way of meditating on the mysteries of Jesus' life, death, and resurrection and as a way of honoring Mary.

✧ The Memorare was one of Elizabeth's favorite prayers. Slowly pray the Memorare, pausing over words and phrases to let their meanings become clear:

> Remember, O most gracious Virgin Mary, that never was it known that anyone who fled to your protection, implored your help, or sought your intercession was left unaided. Inspired with this confidence, we fly unto you, O Virgin of virgins, our Mother! To you we come, before you we stand, sinful and sorrowful. O Mother of the Word incarnate, despise not our petitions, but in your mercy hear and answer us. Amen.

Now make these petitions known to Mary, Mother. Tell her of the graces that you need from Jesus.

✧ Relax your body and mind. If you need to stretch out any kinks in your body, do so. Breathe deeply and slowly. Then bring to mind the kitchen and breakfast table of your childhood home; recall exactly what they looked like. Imagine Mary sitting at the table, having some tea or coffee. You walk through the door, needing to talk about a serious issue, some worry that is gnawing at you. Mary beckons you to sit down, pours you a cup, and says, "What's up? You look like you need to talk." Open your heart and mind to her. Remember, Mary is the mother of love.

God's Word

On the third day there was a wedding at Cana in Galilee. The mother of Jesus was there, and Jesus and his disciples had also been invited. And they ran out of wine, since the wine provided for the feast had all been used, and the mother of Jesus said to him, "They have no wine." Jesus said, "Woman, what do you want from me? My hour has not come yet." His mother said to the servants, "Do whatever he tells you." (John 2:1–5)

Closing prayer: "Blessed Lord, grant me that Humility and Love which has crowned her for Eternity. Happy, happy Blessed Mother, You are united to Him whose absence was your desolation—pity me—pray for me. It is my sweet consolation to think You are pleading for the Wretched poor banished Wanderer" (Kelly and Melville, *Selected Writings*, pp. 56–57).

Parenting

Theme: Elizabeth founded a religious community and administered and taught in schools, but she viewed her role as a parent as a most important sacred trust.

Opening prayer: "Oh my God, *forgive* what I have been, *correct* what I am, and *direct* what I shall be," as I nurture and guide young people, especially if they are my own children (Kelly and Melville, *Selected Writings*, p. 340).

About Elizabeth

Throughout her correspondence, Elizabeth reveals her affection for and profound commitment to her children. One of the hardest decisions she ever made was to leave her children with others in order to accompany Will to Italy, although at that time it was common for relatives to raise the children of absent family members.

Nevertheless, Elizabeth suffered during the separations from her children and rejoiced upon her return to them. When Julia Scott's husband died, Elizabeth went to be with her friend. Afterward she wrote to Eliza Sadler:

> I have not left her night or day during the excess of her sorrows, and such scenes of terror I have gone through as you nor no one can imagine. 'Tis past. . . . I am once

more home, ten thousand times more delighted with it than before. . . . My precious children stick to me like little burrs, they are so fearful of losing me again; the moment I shake one off one side, another clings on the opposite: nor can I write one word without some sweet interruption. (Dirvin, *Mrs. Seton*, p. 56)

After Will's death, Elizabeth assumed the full weight of single parenthood. In New York, she boarded students and ran a school to support her family. Friends and relatives helped her financially, but making ends meet proved immensely difficult. The moves to Baltimore and Emmitsburg improved her situation only somewhat. Besides the day-to-day uncertainties, her children were growing up, and she had to face all the attendant worries.

Elizabeth's reaction to Anna's first infatuation shows both Elizabeth's worry about and sensitivity to her daughter:

My Annina—that is the pinch—my Annina: so young, so lovely, so innocent, absorbed in all the romance of youthful passion. As I have told you, she gave her heart without my knowledge; and afterwards what could a doting and unhappy mother do but take the part of friend and confidante, dissembling my distress and resolving that— if there was no remedy—to help her at least by my love and pity? (Dirvin, *Mrs. Seton*, p. 232)

The romance ended later, but Elizabeth fretted through it all.

Elizabeth took pleasure in being with her children, but she had few illusions about them. The enjoyment and the realism can be seen in excerpts from two letters:

Yesterday we all—about twenty Sisters and children— dined, that is, ate our cold ham and cream pies, in our grotto in the mountain where we go on Sunday for the Divine Office. Richard joined his mother's side, and love with every mouthful, handing the cup of water from the cool stream with as much grace as an angel. But William contented himself with a wave of his hat and a (promise of seeing me) afterwards. . . .

They are two beings as different as sun and moon. . . .

. . . Richard always a mother's boy! All his desire centers in farm, that he may never quit her. William is the boy of hopes and fears . . . and always talks of roving the world. . . . I trust it will all turn out well; for a more loving and tender heart cannot be imagined—tho' the talents of neither of them are distinguished, which does not disappoint me, knowing well they often ruin their owners. (Dirvin, *Mrs. Seton*, pp. 279–280)

Indeed, both William and Richard struggled to find themselves. Elizabeth tried to help her sons by placing them under the tutelage of the Filicchi family, but both turned out to be unsuited for business. Much to her unease, Elizabeth used her friendships to place William in the U.S. Navy; Richard followed him into the service. Far greater pain came to Elizabeth with the deaths of both Anna and Rebecca. Only her profound faith gave Elizabeth hope for the two boys and pulled her through her grieving.

Pause: Ask yourself: Do I consider parenting a holy path?

Elizabeth's Words

Elizabeth and the sisters at Emmitsburg embraced most of the Rule of the Daughters of Charity from France. But when discussions began about joining the two orders into a single community, Elizabeth had one overriding concern:

By the law of the Church I so much love, I could never take an obligation which interfered with my duties to them [her children], except I had an independent provision and guardian for them, which the whole world could not supply to my judgment of a mother's duty.

Here I stand with hands and eyes both lifted to wait the Adorable Will [of God]. The only word I have to say to every question is: *I am a mother*. Whatever providence awaits me consistent with that plea, I say Amen to it. (Dirvin, *Mrs. Seton*, pp. 304–305)

Reflection

Elizabeth loved her children passionately. While juggling many responsibilities, she kept the welfare of her children as her clear priority. She nursed them in their illnesses, played the piano and led them in song, taught them, assisted them with their careers, and grieved for them. Elizabeth sought to do God's will in all matters and knew beyond questioning that part of God's will for her was that she be a wise and loving parent. Motherhood was her ministry and a path to holiness that God chose for her. Parenting can be a path to holiness for all mothers and fathers who love their children.

✧ Ponder your own feelings and attitudes about parenting. Do you see it as a way to holiness?

✧ Reflect on and write your responses to these questions in your journal.
For parents:
✦ Where does parenting actually fit in the list of my priorities?
✦ How much time do I spend with my children each day? Each week?
✦ How well do I really understand my children?
✦ How could I be a better parent?
For non-parents:
✦ Is caring for young people a value for me?
✦ How can I be a mentor or helper to young people?
✦ What can I do to support and encourage parents?

✧ As you slowly and repeatedly pray these words of Mother Seton, bring to mind situations in which you are called to act as a mother or father, older sister or brother, to people—especially children—needing your support, affirmation, wisdom, or protection: "Oh my God, *forgive* what I have been, *correct* what I am, and *direct* what I shall be."

✧ Elizabeth did her best to provide her children with an appropriate education, sufficient food, a healthy environment, and instruction in her faith. Do an examen of consciousness using these questions; talk to Jesus about your responses:

✦ Do I believe in and support affordable and readily available day care for all children?

✦ What is my attitude about funding prenatal care for poor, pregnant women?

✦ How do I feel about programs that feed needy children? Do I give to food banks or shelters?

✦ Am I supportive of child protection laws?

✦ Do I encourage and take an interest in the religious instruction of the children in my church?

✦ How can I help create an environment that will be healthy and clean for future generations?

✦ Am I willing to pay for better educational opportunities for children?

Meditate on any feelings and issues that these questions raise for you. Bring your concerns before God and pray for God's light.

✧ Pray for your parents and for other people who are trying to do God's will by parenting well.

God's Word

Train children in the right way,
    and when old, they will not stray.
(Proverbs 22:6, NRSV)

As tenderly as parents treat their children,
so Yahweh has compassion on those who fear God.
(Psalm 103:13)

Closing prayer: God, our loving parent, may our world be filled with good parents who love, nourish, and guide our children.

Children of the Church

Theme: Elizabeth's loyalty and respect for the church grew from her conviction that she could best find God there.

Opening prayer: God of all goodness, may I rise above my narrow vision of your will and listen to the wisdom in the church, the people of God.

About Elizabeth

Near death, Elizabeth imparted to her community advice that she considered of great importance. In her view, the most necessary ingredient to assure the young community's unity and perseverance was for the members to hold fast to the church. Able to speak only in short sentences, she said: "Be children of the Church, be children of the Church" (Dirvin, *Mrs. Seton*, p. 453).

Elizabeth's long search for truth lead to her decision to become a Catholic. The journey of her heart to Catholicism took her over rough roads of opposition, but once her heart found a home in the decision, she held fast. On 14 March 1805, she professed her commitment to Catholicism. Her feelings and thoughts about that day are summarized in this letter to her friend Amabilia Filicchi:

I was called to a little room next the altar, and there professed to believe what the *Council of Trent* believes and teaches; laughing with my heart to my Savior, who saw that I knew not what the Council of Trent believed—only that it believed what the Church of God declared to be its belief, and consequently is now *my belief.* For as to going a-walking any more about what all the different people believe, I cannot, being quite tired out—and I came up light at heart and cool of head the first time these many long months—but not without begging Our Lord to wrap my heart deep in that opened side so well described in the beautiful Crucifixion, or lock it up in His little tabernacle, where I shall now rest forever. (Dirvin, *Mrs. Seton,* p. 167)

Elizabeth had come to believe in the real presence of Jesus in the Eucharist and in the historicity of the Catholic church. However, what clinched her decision to move into the Catholic community came from another source. In 1816 she confessed to Father Bruté that her final decision came not so much from intellectual conviction but from the need to decide and then to trust God:

I tell you a secret hidden from my own soul—it is so delicate—that my hatred of opposition, troublesome inquiries, etc., brought me in the Church more than conviction. How often I argued to my fearful, uncertain heart: at all events Catholics must be as safe as any other religion; they say none are safe but themselves—*perhaps it is true.* If not, at all events I shall be [as] safe with them as any other. It is the way of suffering and the cross; for me, that is another point of security. (Dirvin, *Mrs. Seton,* p. 166)

Indeed, she did suffer for the decision, but once she became a Catholic, Elizabeth never looked back.

Living within the structure of church authority did not always prove to be comfortable or simple. For example, not all of the priests who acted as superiors to the new community were competent or sensitive. Elizabeth was obliged to develop political skills to cope with these superiors and, at the same time, continue her strong leadership of the community. When

Father John David was appointed the second superior of the community at Emmitsburg, Elizabeth found herself in sharp disagreement with him. She respected David's authority as superior, but she opposed his attempts to usurp the Sister Servant's [Sister Superior's] authority and to change the rules and customs. Elizabeth tried to resolve issues at the local level, but failing this, she wrote to Archbishop Carroll:

> Sincerely I promised you and really *I have endeavored to do every thing in my power* to bend myself to meet the last appointed Superior in every way . . . yet the *heart is closed,* and when the pen should freely give him the necessary detail and information he requires it stops, and . . . *unconquerable reluctance and diffidence takes place of those dispositions* which ought to influence every action and with every desire to serve God and these excellent beings who surround me I remain motionless and inactive. it is for you my most reverend Father to decide if this is temptation or what it is. (Kelly and Melville, *Selected Writings,* p. 267)

Eventually Father David moved to the missions in Kentucky.

Such conflict did not shake Elizabeth's belief that the Holy Spirit always moves through the church, but she respected her own calling to leadership and responsibility within the church.

Pause: What role does the church play in your relationship with God right now?

Elizabeth's Words

> I thank God for having made me a child of His Church: when you come to this hour you will know what it is to be a child of the Church. (Code, *Daily Thoughts,* January 2)

> Speak, Lord, for Thy servant heareth! Thine hour has struck. From now on, no hesitation, no weakness, no procrastination. Holy Church of God, teach, direct, call to thyself thy child, docile and faithful forevermore. (De Barberey, *Elizabeth Seton,* p. 134)

Reflection

Attentive and faithful membership in the church gave Elizabeth direction, support, challenge, and a sense of security. She recognized that fallible human beings inhabit the church; she honestly acknowledged her own shortcomings and frustrations. Because of her human limitations, she gratefully embraced the Eucharist, the church's heritage, and other means of discerning and doing God's will that are part of church life.

Fidelity to the church can be taxing; the deepest obedience is not always silent. When obedience and loyalty spring truly from love and faith, that love and concern can impel a faithful member to speak out, to call to task, and even at times to confront. Speaking the truth in love, Elizabeth learned, must come from a prayerful discernment of the Spirit and will of God. In any case, Elizabeth would still urge us to be children of the church.

✧ Consider your own commitment to the church. Review your history with the church and outline key experiences in your relationship. Then write your reflections on these questions:
+ In what ways have I found the church a support?
+ How has the church challenged me to be more loving?
+ How have I experienced the Holy Spirit leading me through the church?
+ When has the church provided me with direction or focus for my life?
+ In what ways has the church given me a sense of security?

✧ List any questions, problems, disagreements, or reservations that you have about the church. If a problem comes from lack of information, try to read about the problem in contemporary journals or books. If a disagreement stems from a personal experience, pray about and discern ways of resolving or letting go of the disagreement. Ask for guidance of the Holy Spirit in healing any friction with the church.

✧ Meditate on the ways in which you are responsive to the church. How do you contribute to the building of the Body of Christ? Are there ways in which you could become further involved in your church community?

✧ The church always stands in need of reformation and renewal. Pray that God will grace the people of God with saintly leaders, open hearts, and willing spirits.

✧ Slowly read the section "God's Word," in which Paul writes to the community in Corinth. He is taking up a collection for the famine-stricken church in Jerusalem and giving advice to the Christians of Corinth. How does this image of the church match your own experience? Talk with Jesus about this question.

God's Word

Now about the collection for God's holy people; you are to do the same as I prescribed for the churches in Galatia. On the first day of the week, each of you should put aside and reserve as much as each can spare; . . . When I come, I will send to Jerusalem with letters of introduction those people you approve to deliver your gift. . . .

Be vigilant, stay firm in the faith, be brave and strong. Let everything you do be done in love.

. . . You know how the Stephanas family have been the first-fruits of Achaia and have devoted themselves to the service of God's holy people; I ask you in turn to put yourselves at the service of people like this and all that work with them in this arduous task. . . .

The churches of Asia send their greetings. Aquila and Prisca send their best wishes. . . . Greet one another with the holy kiss.

This greeting is in my own hand—PAUL. (1 Corinthians 16:1–21)

Closing prayer: Spirit of the living God, may I bear my responsibility to your people, the church, in loyalty, with inspired vision, and in gratitude and joy.

✧ **Meditation 15** ✧

Hope in the Resurrection

Theme: Elizabeth's faith in and love for God buttressed her hope for eternal life, and belief in the final resurrection gave her the courage to go on.

Opening prayer: Holy Friend, grant that I may hold fast to my hope in rising to eternal life with you.

About Elizabeth

Death claimed her husband, several of her closest friends, many of the founding sisters in the community, and two of her children before it finally claimed Elizabeth. Pain and sorrow in many other forms frequently knocked at the door of Elizabeth's heart, but she knew that she had to carry on, looking up. She knew that at the last, all tears would be wiped away.

The death of her daughter Anna almost drove Elizabeth into despair. She told a friend, "For three months after Nina was taken I was so often expecting to lose my senses, and my head was so disordered" (Dirvin, *Mrs. Seton*, p. 320). In a letter to another friend, her grief continued to pour out:

> If you could have seen at the moment when kneeling at the foot of her bed to rub her cold, cold feet a day or two before—she saw the tears, and without being able to hide

her own, tho' smiling at the same time, she repeated the so-often-asked question:

"Can it be for me? Should you not rejoice? It will be but a moment, and reunited for Eternity. A happy eternity with my Mother—what a thought!"

These were her very words. And when in death's agony her quivering lips could with difficulty utter one word, feeling a tear fall on her face, she smiled and said with great effort: *"Laugh, Mother, Jesus!"*—at intervals, as she could not put two words together. . . .

Poor Mother must say no more now; only pray, Eliza, that she may be strengthened. . . . You believe me when I say with my whole soul, "His Will be done forever!" (Dirvin, *Mrs. Seton,* p. 321)

The grief over Anna's death finally eased, leaving Elizabeth peace and hope in eternal life with her loved ones. To her dear friend Julia Scott, Elizabeth confided:

I sit writing by the window, opposite my darling darling's *little Wood.* The white palings appear thro' the trees. Oh, Julia, my Julia, if we may but pass our dear eternity together! . . . I long so to get above this blue horizon. Oh, my Anna, the child of my soul! All, all dear ones so many years gone before! ETERNAL REUNION! (Dirvin, *Mrs. Seton,* p. 335)

Elizabeth found it useless to dwell on past or future problems over which she had no control, saying, "What is sorrow, what is death? They are but sounds when at peace with Jesus. Sorrow and death—their real sense is the loss of His dear love" (De Barberey, *Elizabeth Seton,* p. 201). She used the hard lessons learned to soften her own heart and to better understand and help others.

Pause: Ponder this question: Do I trust in God's promise of eternal life?

Elizabeth's Words

Let them plough, let them grind; so much the better, the grain will be sooner prepared for its owner; whereas, should I step forward and take my own cause in hand, the Father of the widow and the orphan would say I distrust Him. . . . Shall we make schemes and plans of human happiness, which must be so uncertain in obtaining, and if obtained—hush—death! eternity! Oh, my father, *sursum corda*—we know better than to be cheated by such attractions. No, we will offer the hourly sacrifice, and drink our cup to the last drop, and we, when least expecting it, will enter into our rest. (Charles I. White, *Mother Seton*, p. 271)

Do we serve God in Hope, looking to his promises, confiding in his love, seeking his Kingdom, and leaving the rest to him—do we rely on his merits his pains his sufferings fulfilling our common duties in union with him—our contrition united to his contrition our tears to his tears, looking forward to the time when he will appear, when we shall see him as he is, see him in his glory, and be glorified with him—rejoicing in Hope!—for Hope shall never be confounded. (Kelly and Melville, *Selected Writings*, p. 326)

Reflection

The giant sequoia tree can survive forest fires burning fiercely inside the trunk. The gap eventually heals, but a blackened hollow scar, visible even hundreds of years later, gives a vivid reminder of the torment it has endured.

Many of our wounds have left scars on us, perhaps invisible to the eye, but real all the same. After all, even a small thorn in our finger can cause throbbing pain and may mark us. We can learn to live with these thorns and scars even as Elizabeth did, especially if we have hope in the promise of eternal life. The promise of the resurrection never served Mother Seton as an excuse for inaction. Rather, it urged her to keep serving, praying, and hoping, because a loving God would ultimately provide peace and rest.

✧ Read "Elizabeth's Words" once again. Then reflect on the following statements. If you find it helpful, write down your reactions:

✦ When I imagine my own dying, I imagine . . .
✦ When I think of death, I . . .
✦ When I picture what happens after death, I picture . . .

Share your thoughts and feelings with Jesus. Open your heart to him, especially about any of your fears.

✧ People in Elizabeth's time did not expect to live long. They died of illnesses and diseases that are easily cured today, so death's reality stared them in the face much more frequently. Has anyone close to you died? If so, recall their dying. What feelings did you have at the time? How did the person approach his or her death? What solace did you have in your grieving?

✧ List all the people with whom you hope to share what Mother Seton called ETERNAL REUNION! Thank God for these people; offer their names to God. Then meditate on how you can be more closely united to those people still living and how you can live in the spirit of those already gone before you.

. If you have not visited the graves of your deceased loved ones in some time, try to do so. When you make your visit, thank God for your loved ones. Ponder how they enriched your life and ask God for the grace you need to live in a manner worthy of these loved ones.

✧ Find a quiet place to kneel. Raise your arms and open your hands towards heaven, praying slowly and repeatedly: Hope in God shall never be confounded! Then unite your spirit with Elizabeth's by offering thanks to God for love.

God's Word

We want you to be quite certain . . . about those who
have fallen asleep, to make sure that you do not grieve for
them, as others do who have no hope. We believe that
Jesus died and rose again, and that in the same way God
will bring [back] those who have fallen asleep in Jesus.
(1 Thessalonians 4:13–14)

Closing prayer:

the sleep and dream of life
—the awakening to another life
the horizon of futurity
the pure skies of heaven
dawning of Eternity
Rising sun of Immortality
splendor
beauty
perfumes
angelic singing
views immense
Jesus—infinity itself
boundless light
all delight
all bliss
all GOD
all this may be tomorrow
if only from the sleep
and dreams
of life
I may
through penance
and innocence
truly awake in Jesus!!!
(Kelly and Melville, *Selected Writings*, pp. 339–340)

F·RI·EN·D

✧ For Further Reading ✧

De Barberey, Madame [Helen Bailly]. *Elizabeth Seton*. Translated and adapted from the sixth French edition by Joseph B. Code. New York: Macmillan, 1927.

De Pauw, Linda Grant. *Founding Mothers: Women of America in the Revolutionary Era*. Boston: Houghton-Mifflin, 1975.

Dirvin, Joseph I. *Mrs. Seton: Foundress of the American Sisters of Charity*. New York: Farrar, Straus and Giroux, 1962.

———. *The Soul of Elizabeth Seton*. San Francisco: Ignatius Press, 1990.

Kelly, Ellin, and Annabelle M. Melville, eds. *Elizabeth Seton: Selected Writings*. New York: Paulist Press, 1987.

Laverty, Rose Maria. *Loom of Many Threads: The English and French Influences on the Character of Elizabeth Ann Bayley Seton*. New York: Paulist Press, 1958.

Melville, Annabelle M. *Elizabeth Bayley Seton, 1774–1821*. New preface edition. New York: Charles Scribner's Sons, 1976.

Titles in the Companions for the Journey Series

Order from your local religious bookstore or from

Saint Mary's Press
702 TERRACE HEIGHTS
WINONA MN 55987-1320
USA
800-533-8095
www.smp.org